DATE DUE

DEMCO 38-296

FAIR
AND EFFECTIVE
EMPLOYMENT TESTING

Recent Titles from Quorum Books

FAIR AND EFFECTIVE EMPLOYMENT TESTING

Administrative, Psychometric, and Legal Issues for the Human Resources Professional

Wilfredo R. Manese

Q

QUORUM BOOKS

NEW YORK • WESTPORT, CONNECTICUT • LONDON

Library of Congress Cataloging-in-Publication Data

Manese, Wilfredo R.
  Fair and effective employment testing.

  Bibliography: p.
  Includes index.
  1. Employment tests. I. Title.
HF5549.5.E5M29   1986   658.3'1125   85-27151
ISBN 0-89930-171-1 (lib. bdg. : alk. paper)

Library of Congress Catalog Card Number: 85-27151
ISBN: 0-89930-171-1

First published in 1986 by Quorum Books

Greenwood Press, Inc.
88 Post Road West, Westport, Connecticut 06881

Printed in the United States of America

The paper used in this book complies with the
Permanent Paper Standard issued by the National
Information Standards Organization (Z39.48-1984).

10 9 8 7 6 5 4 3 2 1

To the memory of my parents

CONTENTS

PART II. EMPLOYMENT TESTING—
THE PSYCHOMETRIC CONTEXT

PART III.   EMPLOYMENT TESTING—
THE LEGAL CONTEXT

PREFACE

This book was written to provide a source of practical guidance to the use of employment tests. For as long as selection decisions are made, employment tests will be seen as a potential source of relevant information for determining which applicants should be rejected and which ones should be accepted. The idea that employment tests are useful personnel tools is still widely entertained even though events over the last few years since the passage of the Civil Rights Act of 1964 may have shaken the strength with which the idea is held. The utility of employment tests may have been obscured by the debate over whether tests are biased against minorities or whether the tests stand in the way of meeting an organization's affirmative action commitments. Some bad press attended the first testing cases that were decided in various legal forums against test-using employers. Matters were not helped any by the issuance, in fairly close succession, of a number of federal testing guidelines (6 in the last 14 years) which left employers anxious and confused. At one point, between November 1976 and September 1978, 2 sets of testing guidelines with nonidentical provisions were issued by various agencies of the federal government.

The clouds of ambiguity have begun to lift: The case law on testing and employment discrimination is more settled after such landmark cases as *Griggs v. Duke Power Co.* (3 FEP 175 (1971)), *Albemarle Paper Co. et al. v.*

Moody et al. (10 FEP 1181 (1975)), and *Washington et al. v. Davis et al.* (12 FEP 1415 (1976)). On the research side, F. Schmidt and J. Hunter (1981) paved the way for the sort of programmatic studies that have established that testing devices are valid for and fair to both minorities and nonminorities. The various federal agencies provided clarity when they decided to speak with 1 tongue in the form of 1 uniform set of federal guidelines on the use of tests and other selection procedures. It seems fair to say that the Civil Rights Act of 1964 triggered vigorous activities in various circles—academic, governmental, and legal—that led to an accelerated resolution of what, in retrospect, now appear as transitional issues.

The impact of the foregoing developments on testing is twofold. First, employment testing is now a multidisciplinary enterprise. The psychologist who develops or validates the test, the test specialist who administers and scores the test, the lawyer who is called upon to defend the test's use against charges of unlawful employment discrimination, and the manager who must juggle the advantages and disadvantages of using tests to meet the staffing requirements and affirmative action commitments of the business— all are in it together, drawn by the reality that an employment test is at once a measuring instrument, a management device for managing applicant flow, a prediction tool for making hiring decisions, and a potential cause of action for plaintiffs alleging discrimination. The second consequence follows from the first. The multidisciplinary character of employment testing calls for a more expansive, less provincial approach to what testing is about. Treatises on the subject become more useful to the extent that the major psychometric, legal, and administrative aspects are covered in terms that can be understood by an audience that has grown heterogeneous in technical expertise. The present work was written in an attempt to fill this bill, to capture as much of the full picture as possible using language that is neither esoteric nor simplistic.

There is a slight bias to my writing. Of the principal players involved in the development and use of testing devices, the psychologist, the statistician, and the lawyer are schooled in disciplines that give them the technical/professional wherewithal to crunch the data. The same facility cannot be assumed for the typical test taker or the typical test user. Accordingly, we have kept the needs of these last 2 groups prominently in mind. To elaborate: How has the typical job candidate been affected by the changes and how does he react to them? (The masculine pronoun is used throughout the book solely for convenience rather than to indicate gender.) He notices that employment offices are decked with posters announcing the different antidiscrimination laws and the company's announced intention to comply with all of them. Because the posters must be displayed in conspicuous places, it is difficult for him not to notice them. He may also have read in the papers about some of the landmark cases such as *Griggs, Albemarle, Bakke,* and *Weber.* There may have been others—the names have a way of running together after a while. Someday he hopes to be enough of a lawyer, personnel manager, statistician, and industrial psychologist to figure out what employment testing and those amorphous "EEO [equal employment opportunity] considerations" are all about. In the meantime, his level of consciousness about these matters has been raised. It may be some time, however, before he is able to sort out the relevant developments into a coherent framework that he can understand. There seem to be too many disjointed strands: personnel tests that ask him questions about the darnedest things that have no discernible relationship to the job that he is applying for; government agencies that remind him of his many rights but do so in bureaucratic gobbledygook that leaves him bewildered; court decisions written in such ponderous language that leaves him dazzled but uncomprehending; and the personal experiences of friends recounted in so many versions that he is unable to separate the wheat from the chaff. All in all, the typical job candidate feels a bit overwhelmed by the complexity of the developments and somewhat frustrated, if not resentful, that he is unable to participate more actively in influencing events that intrude on his chances of obtaining gainful employment.

The typical employment manager may not be in any better shape. On any given day, he may be called upon to translate into layman terms such technical concepts as test validity (he could try to be clever and start out by using the analogy of getting one's parking ticket validated) or to answer questions pertaining to the latest regulation on the handicapped (sooner or later, he is convinced that everybody is going to be covered by one law or another) or to prepare testimony for an arbitration case (everyone seems to be wanting a piece of the action)—all the while attending to the goals and timetables mandated by Revised Order No. 4. Personnel jobs have ceased to be the cushy assignments they once were, he concludes.

It is tempting and not too difficult to leave the typical test taker and test user to their own bewilderments about testing matters. Most traditional offerings, whether in the form of conferences, workshops, or standard textbooks, can be faulted either for their limited and narrow treatment of the subject or for their attempts to cover the waterfront but at a level of discourse that is several notches over the head of the nontechnical person. If the present work departs from traditional approaches, it is in the direction that takes the nontechnical readership's needs into account. Of particular concern to us is the manager who plays a key role in determining whether and the extent to which he will use tests to meet the human resources requirements of the enterprise. The manager's realities are more urgent than those that face the academician or the bureaucrat. He needs to make selection decisions and he will need to do so with or without the benefit of employment tests. His responsibilities cannot be put on hold to await the final iteration of the federal guidelines on testing nor can they be discharged intelligently without access to the fundamentals of the testing enterprise in the context of today's realities. The manager needs a source of general guidance, a sort of rough map of the constraints and the opportunities, packaged "to go"—without the trimmings and nuances of standard textbook offerings. I have structured the content and the format of the book to be responsive to the manager's needs and, by extension, to the needs of other consumers of testing services. If the attempt is successful, I will have met a personal objective: Food that is packaged to go does not have to be watered down!

The nontraditional character of the present offering can be made more explicit by pointing out the following features:

1. The focus is on the more applied aspects of employment testing. If the distinction between test development and test usage is a viable one, this book concentrates on concepts more closely associated with test usage issues. Test development efforts are directed at the internal characteristics of the test (for example, test content or clarity of the test items), while test usage issues address the more contextual factors: the social, business, and legal consequences flowing from acting on test results to arrive at personnel decisions. Test specialists may refer to these applied aspects of testing as the more mundane aspects of the trade and may have, on that account, not given them the extended treatment in standard texts that is typically accorded to the more technical aspects of psychological measurement.

2. The book is written for an audience that is vitally interested in the more mundane aspects of employment testing. With little or no formal training in psychological measurement, the typical reader is a consumer of testing services who has a need for a practical knowledge of what employment testing is about. Phrases like "seeing the big picture" or "hitting the high points" describe his goal of getting the story straight without all the trimmings. He has no particular interest in the technicalities that he views, with some resignation, as best reserved for standard textbooks.

3. The book is written as nontechnically as possible. There are times when technical terms cannot be avoided or when technical accuracy calls for a level of explanation above the plane of everyday language. These have been kept to a minimum.

4. The bulk of the book is written in question-and-answer (Q and A) format. The questions are numbered consecutively for ease in cross-referencing. The Q and A approach is more earthy, forcing the presentation of information in bite-size modules. I suspect that this format best meets the needs of the typical reader who sees the world of testing as a series of discrete, stand-alone issues rather than as a rigorously ordered body of knowledge and who operates in the same mode when seeking or dispensing information on testing matters. That is to say, I believe that the Q and A format, rather than the standard textbook approach, suitably meets my readership's a la carte requirements for information.

In terms of content, the book aims to take in the major contemporary and interactive influences that impinge on the field of employment testing. Two introductory sections precede the Q and A section. The intent of these sections is to provide the reader with a working knowledge of the big picture before I cut up the turf into the yards and inches of the Qs and As. The first section is in the nature of a status report on employment testing today, beginning with some survey results pertaining to the incidence of test use followed by a look at suitable alternatives to paper-and-pencil testing devices and a summary of the programmatic research on the issues of differential validity, test fairness, and validity generalization. The second section is a step-by-step treatment of the procedures involved in performing a validation study. Each step is discussed from a technical as well as a practitioner's point of view.

The Q and A portion, which represents the bulk of the book, is organized into 3 parts. Part I deals with questions that fall within the domain of the test-taking manager or lay practitioner's everyday world. Some representative questions include: *How are tests used in the employment process? Will employment testing hurt affirmative action efforts? How are passing scores set? What are the consequences of using an invalid test? Is it better to validate a test or minimize its adverse impact?*

Part II is more psychometric in nature. It deals with the meaning of test validity and the different ways of interpreting the outcome of validation studies and addresses questions pertaining to test fairness.

Part III presents the more legalistic side of employment testing. The major concepts that have been associated with testing and equal opportunity law, such as adverse impact, the so-called 4/5ths rule, the bottom-line concept, job relatedness, and the Equal Employment Opportunity Commission's (EEOC) role in the enforcement of antidiscrimination are covered as well as the landmark testing cases that have been decided by the U.S. Supreme Court.

A few caveats:

1. The book is definitely not a do-it-yourself kit on how to validate personnel tests and other employee selection procedures. Test validation, already an arduous technical undertaking, has taken on a legal character in recent years. As a consequence, the testing enterprise has become pervasively regulated. In earlier times, the nonspecialist who conducted a homegrown validation study might be regarded as something of an entrepreneur worthy of admiration or envy. The same individual today would be seen as walking a tightrope without a net and likely to be regarded as possessed of reckless tendencies.

2. The book concentrates on well-settled principles and developments or, where appropriate, provides a summary of major research trends. As a general rule, if a particular topic cannot be accurately described without strenuous qualifications, it is probably not covered in this book.

3. Sooner or later, the book will reach questions that are emotionally loaded or that call for answers that are not too popular. I approach these issues by heeding the admonition of the young to "tell it like it is."

Every piece of writing communicates a point of view. The present work is no exception. I propose a more managerial approach to the use of tests for employment purposes. The managerial perspective goes beyond psychometric considerations; it manages the testing enterprise, discerning opportunities amidst legal constraints, and seeing no inherent contradiction between meeting affirmative action commitments and testing for competency. My perspective suggests that, after the dust settles and group differences in test performance—their origins and their consequences—have been studied, quantified, and litigated, it remains for competent management to take it from here in the service of using test results to meet the human requirements of the business.

The managerial perspective that I urge does not reflect any disillusionment with traditional approaches to testing as exemplified, for example, by A. Jensen's (1980) book *Bias in Mental Testing*. There will always be a place for a good book on psychological measurement or a competently done validation study. Treatises on racial differences in test performance, like a good Bogart movie, will always attract a following (no matter how late the hour). Understanding the technical aspects involved in matching worker characteristics with job requirements is a necessary first step in the competent management of human resources. It does not have to be the last step. Events over the last few years have made it clear that if we are to meet the full spectrum of issues and challenges in the area of human resource utilization, we must be prepared to go beyond the mechanics of test validation. We need to put employment testing in its rightful place—a personnel tool whose use requires an understanding of what it can and can't do. Necessarily, we must cast the net wide to reach the many constituencies whose concerns need to be represented. It is because my target audience has grown and grown more diverse and it is because the issues go beyond validation that this book was written the way it was. Pogo may have captured my sentiments more succinctly when he mused that "the future is not what it used to be."

It is customary to end this part of the book with acknowledgments of gratitude to those who supported the author's efforts. Most frequently, the acknowledgment goes to those who shouldered the extra load as the author dropped out of the daily routine in order to work on the manuscript. My lovely wife, Evelyn, and our two boys, Eric and Paul, fall under this category and I thank them for their patience and understanding. With the completion of the work, I now have an answer to Eric's question of when I might get done. Paul's question, why it took so long, will remain in rhetorical limbo for a while longer. The bulk of the present book was prepared while I was on special assignment to a team charged with developing a job evaluation plan with our union colleagues. Although our collaborative endeavor dealt with a subject that was different from what is covered in this book, my piece of the action was clearly defined. It was thus possible to work on the manuscript at night after having "given at the office" during the day. Accordingly, under a separate category that I label "other," I acknowledge my colleagues and work associates in what was then one Bell System. Finally, under the category labelled "very special," I acknowledge with respect and admiration the lifelong support and encouragement provided by 2 very wonderful people—my mom and dad—who were both killed in an automobile accident while this book was in preparation. To both of them, I am honored to dedicate this book.

*FAIR
AND EFFECTIVE
EMPLOYMENT TESTING*

THE CASE FOR EMPLOYMENT TESTING

This introductory section looks at the case for employment testing. Recent survey data that bear on the incidence of test usage are examined. Test usage is wide and pervasive: Tests are used in the private, public, and military sectors to make generic employment decisions involving the selection, placement, and classification of personnel. Next examined is research evidence on the efficacy of devices other than traditional paper-and-pencil employment tests and recent developments pertaining to the fairness, utility, and generalizability of employment tests. The findings indicate that employment tests are equally valid for and fair to minority and nonminority groups and yield practical payoffs that may have been underestimated. The case for employment testing is a strong one: Properly validated paper-and-pencil employment tests provide an efficient, cost-effective mechanism for meeting the human requirements of the business and there are few suitable alternatives that will do the job. The section concludes by calling attention to the changing character of employment testing. A test is at once a psychometric device for measuring job-relevant characteristics, a management tool for making selection decisions among job candidates, and an exhibit in a legal proceeding alleging that the test is unfairly discriminatory. This expanded view of employment testing is timely and salutary.

DEFINITION OF AN EMPLOYMENT TEST

Most applicants for employment would identify an employment test as some sort of paper-and-pencil device that measures a particular skill, knowledge, or ability from the domain of job requirements. The questions in the test are typically cast in a multiple-choice format where the examinee indicates his answers from among the alternatives proffered by blackening or "bubbling in" the corresponding spots in a separate answer sheet. The directions in the test booklet instruct the examinees to spend the allotted time judiciously, to use a number 2 pencil for recording their responses, and to erase completely any answer they wish to change. Scoring of the test is accomplished by superimposing on the answer sheet a template that has been pre-punched with the correct answers and by counting off the number of correct responses. The test is suitable for group administration: It can be given to a group of examinees at the same time, making it possible to obtain test scores on a number of examinees in 1 testing session.

The foregoing characterization of an employment test is a familiar one. It is not very different from the SAT (Scholastic Aptitude Test), the GRE (Graduate Record Examinations), and similar examinations developed for use in the academic setting. There are, of course, other kinds of examinations used for selecting, placing, and counseling students, just as there are other types of selection techniques that are used in the employment context. The focus of this work is on the traditional paper-and-pencil employment test. In addition to being widely known, traditional employment tests provide an identifiable body of folklore and scholarly studies, misconceptions and accepted principles, concepts, and practices that make them a convenient point of departure for discussion. Where the focus is deviated from, it is to recognize the more expansive definition of tests contained in the *Uniform Guidelines on Employee Selection Procedures* (EEOC, 1978), to examine the viability of nontest measures that have been advanced as potential suitable alternatives, or to discuss the other components of the selection process. It is clear, however, that conventional paper-and-pencil tests represent the mainstream and focusing on them provides the link of continuity between the present work and other treatises and texts on the subject.

Other Aspects of Employment Testing

Employment tests are seen by various segments of the general population as representing more than measuring devices that register scores on some aptitude or skill requirement. Some see employment tests as indispensable management tools for efficiently sorting job candidates into qualified and nonqualified categories. Relatively inexpensive and appearing "scientific" on their face, employment tests provide a quick screening device for determining the qualifications of people from all walks of life and from a wide variety of cultural backgrounds. Just the sort of thing we need, practitioners insist, to manage the flow of candidates to the more expensive modules of the employment process, such as the evaluation interview, the medical evaluation, or reference/security/credit checks. Others view employment tests as powerful gatekeepers to equality of economic opportunity and object to the overemphasis given to test scores in determining who gets hired and who does not. They observe that something is wrong with a society where one's livelihood or one's career depends on a single number— his test score. With measured cynicism, these others also point to the impersonal interaction between examinee and test administrator as indicative of a workplace grown numb to the nuances of human individuality. What is needed, it is argued, is an assessment of the whole person on a 1-to-1 basis. A more extreme view sees employment tests as subtle mechanisms that operate to perpetuate the effects of historical disparities between racial and/or sex groups. Charges of racism or sexism are not far behind.

There are several reasons for the mixed reactions to employment testing. There is, first, an aura of mystique that pervades the measurement of personal characteristics. Visions of Rorschach inkblot tests of personality are evoked by the mention of psychological tests. Vaguely mysterious, psychological tests titillate the popular mind that does not sharply or clearly draw the distinction between tests in general and tests used to arrive at personnel decisions in the employment context. If psychological tests are painted with less than favorable colors, employment tests tend to be tainted with the same brush. Second, employment testing is embedded in a discipline that is young, evolving, and, by some standards, fairly inexact. Test specialists communicate in technical language, using probabilistic statements that strike the lay person as being too tentative to provide guidance to questions of social policy. What is overlooked is the reality that research activities generate answers to scientific hypotheses, not solutions to pressing social issues. Stated differently, social policy decisions require that the outcome of research endeavors be interpreted within a framework of values that go beyond considerations of professional rigor or statistical significance. Third, discussions of employment testing have a way of provoking discussions of unfair discrimination (as when tests are implicated in the slow utilization of minorities in the work force) or reverse discrimination (as when low-scoring minorities are hired in order to implement affirmative action programs)—concepts that are linked to one's daily bread. The discussions are hardly dispassionate and, in due course, employment testing is drowned in the heated debate of what is right and what is wrong with the American scene. Last, there are inevitable incidents of test abuse. A few of these may trigger court action; most frequently, the aggrieved chalks it up to experience and silently harbors a profound distrust of the employer by whom he feels disenfranchised and of the instrument (test) that was involved in the process. Explanations from test publishers to the effect that reported deviations from sound professional practice do not exceed what could be expected to occur by chance are not reassuring; in the minds of some, they are downright irrelevant. How does one cope with isolated instances of test abuse, whether these are experienced personally or vicariously through such popular writings as M. Gross' *The Brain Watchers* (1962) or B. Hoffman's *The Tyranny of Testing* (1962)? The question has its counterparts in the medical field where a doctor is sued for malpractice not for the 999 successful operations but for the 1 instance of professional inadvertence.

INCIDENCE OF TEST USE

Selection decisions are made every day to meet staffing requirements in both the private (business), public (civilian government), and military segments of the economy. How many of the decisions involving the initial intake of personnel and the subsequent internal movements of employees are made with the help of information provided by employment tests? A report prepared by T. Friedman and E. B. Williams (1980) for the National Academy of Sciences presents a summary of the incidence of test use in each of the 3 employment sectors.

The message of the Friedman and Williams report is clear: employment testing is a significant activity in each of the 3 major sections of the workforce. Some of the numbers cited in the report drive the point home:

- 49.1% of the 1,339 respondents in the survey conducted in 1975 by Prentice Hall and the American Society for Personnel Administration (ASPA) used tests for hiring;
- 42% of the Bureau of National Affairs (BNA) survey sample of 196 personnel executives who were polled in 1976 reported giving pre-employment tests to prospective employees;
- in the federal government, 63 different standardized tests are used as one of the threshold requirements for filling entry-level positions in approximately 300 occupations (In fiscal year 1978, close to 700,000 applicants were administered written tests.);
- in a 1970 survey of 45 state, 110 county and 202 municipal units, test use for hiring purposes was found to range from 35% of the respondents (for hiring of unskilled workers) to 88% of the respondents (for hiring entry-level office workers);
- in the military sector, the Armed Services Vocational Aptitude Battery (ASVAB)— implemented in 1976 as a single test battery for Department of Defense-wide use—was administered to almost a million high school students during the 1978-1979 school year to determine their eligibility for military enlistment.

Other items of interest from the Friedman and Williams survey include the following:

1. The incidence of test use in the private sector is correlated with the size of the employer: The bigger the company, the more likely it is to use tests.

2. In both the BNA and the Prentice Hall/ASPA surveys, the job categories showing the heaviest testing activity were the office or clerical job classifications—usually the high incumbency, high turnover, entry-level categories. This finding and the previously cited finding that shows that test use rises with the size of the company are not surprising since it is the large employer who can be expected to show greater employment activity and who needs the cost-effective mechanism of a testing program to manage the flow of job candidates to the more expensive modules of the employment process.

3. Among test-using companies, the information provided by tests is considered along with the information provided by other modules in the employment process in arriving at a final selection decision. Thus, test scores are rarely a knock-out factor in determining job suitability.

4. There are indications of a decline in testing activity as a result of the passage of antidiscrimination legislation. The number of organizations continuing to use tests, however, remains substantial.

ALTERNATIVES TO CONVENTIONAL TESTS

Are there alternatives to conventional employment tests? How do these alternatives stack up against conventional employment tests on such dimensions as validity, adverse impact, and fairness? R. R. Reilly and G. Chao (1982) sought answers to these questions by examining 8 categories of alternative selection procedures. They found promise for 2 of the 8 categories (biodata and peer evaluations) in terms of validity but there are technical and practical problems associated with their operational use.

Reilly and Chao defined a conventional test as "a standardized measure of aptitude, knowledge, ability, personality or performance with fixed rules for administration and scoring" (p. 4). This definition tracks closely with the definition of employment tests in this book.

Information on alternatives to conventional tests was obtained from 3 sources: a survey of the membership of Division 14 (Division of Industrial and Organizational Psychology); articles published in the *Journal of Applied Psychology* and *Personnel Psychology* predominantly during the 1970-1979 time frame; and a computer search of technical reports prepared for governmental funding agencies. For a particular study to be included in the Reilly and Chao review, it had to meet a number of technical criteria. For example, only studies reporting empirical relationships between the scores on the alternative predictors and on the criterion measures of occupational performance were reviewed. The studies ending up being included in the Reilly and Chao list represent better quality studies in terms of their adherence to commonly accepted principles of experimental design and professional practice.

The alternative selection procedures fall into 1 of 8 categories that are listed and described below:

1. *Biographical information or biodata.* Items of biographical or personal history information are collected through an employment application blank or a form resembling a conventional test booklet. Based on the rationale that the best predictor of future performance is past performance, biodata seek to identify those demographic and work history characteristics that are indicative of occupational success.

2. *Interview.* The interview is the most widely used selection procedure and involves a face-to-face interaction between the job candidate and a representative of the employing organization.

3. *Peer evaluations.* Evaluative judgments about a job candidate obtained from a coworker peer.

4. *Self-assessments.* Self-reports of an applicant's ability, skill, or knowledge.

5. *Reference checks.* Testimonials about an applicant's suitability that are obtained from previous employers.

6. *Academic performance measures.* Measures of how well a person did in school that are frequently condensed into such indices as grade point average (GPA) or rank in class.

7. *Expert judgment.* Evaluative opinions from such expert judges as consultants or those with experience in the particular occupation sought by the job candidate.

8. *Projective techniques.* Techniques that call for the examinee to respond to unstructured and ambiguous stimuli, such as inkblots, and that are used to measure the motivational and personality characteristics of job candidates.

For each alternative selection procedure, Reilly and Chao examined its level of validity, adverse impact, and fairness. As a general rule, data pertaining to adverse impact and fairness were more limited than the data reported for the procedure's validity level. Furthermore, proxy definitions were adopted for adverse impact and fairness in order to accommodate the data. Adverse impact, normally defined in terms of differences in selection rates between subgroups, was inferred from statistically significant differences in mean scores on the selection procedure. Similarly, assessment of a procedure's fairness, normally made by comparing subgroup errors of estimate, slopes, and intercepts, was tested by comparing subgroup validity coefficients. In general, the proxy assessments of adverse impact and fairness that Reilly and Chao adopted represent very reasonable approaches to accommodate the sorts of data that they had to work with.

The average validity for biodata was .35 for the studies reviewed by Reilly and Chao. This level of validity compares favorably with the average validities of .20 and .30 reported by E. Ghiselli (1966) for conventional tests against job proficiency and training criteria, respectively. The limited data on adverse impact and the even more limited data on fairness indicate that biodata are little different on these dimensions from conventional tests. Reilly and Chao concluded that biodata represent good candidates for suitable alternatives to conventional tests. They did sound a cautionary note: The validity of empirically keyed biodata scores tends to diminish over time, making it necessary to periodically revalidate empirically derived keys. To elaborate, biodata forms (also called biodata inventories or biographical questionnaires), unlike conventional aptitude tests, do not have *a priori* correct responses. The "correct" answers are developed based on empirical data that indicate that a particular item alternative differentiates between known groups. In a validation study, the known groups might consist of individuals designated as successful (Group X) according to their scores on some criterion measure of job performance and of their less successful counterparts (Group Y). Extensive statistical analyses are performed on the responses of the 2 groups to each item of the biodata inventory. In the end, those items and item alternatives are identified or "keyed" that are able to differentiate between the two groups. A scoring key is empirically derived that consists of the specific subset of items and item alternatives responded to differently (at some specified level of statistical significance) by Group X and Group Y. Two illustrative items from a hypothetical response matrix are shown below. It is assumed that Group X is the more successful group. The percentages that are tabulated show the proportion within each group that selected each item alternative.

Item 7: When you were growing up, how much attention did your parents give you?

	Group X	Group Y
1. a whole lot	20%	22%
2. a good bit	20%	20%
3. some	20%	18%
4. little	20%	20%
5. very little	20%	20%

Item 20: How interested were your parents in activities in which you engaged?

	Group X	Group Y
1. very much	20%	25%
2. much	45%	25% (statistically significant)
3. some	20%	30%
4. little	10%	13%
5. very little	5%	7%

It will be seen that the 2 groups responded to Item 7 in about the same way; none of the item alternatives would be keyed. This is not the case for Item 20, where alternative 2 was selected significantly more frequently by Group X than by the less successful members of Group Y. Alternative 2 would thus be keyed. Each item alternative in a biodata inventory would be analyzed in this fashion to identify the subset of item alternatives that empirically differentiate between known criterion groups. To be sure that the obtained differentiations hold up, it is customary to apply the empirically derived scoring key to another independent sample in a study known as cross-validation. If the scoring key is able to differentiate between the more and the less successful members of this independent sample, the scoring key is ready for operational use.

The concept of cross-validation is different from the concept of revalidation. Whereas cross-validation involves checking results across study samples, the concept of revalidation involves checking the stability of empirically derived keys at various points in time. Cross-validation is a safeguard against differentiations that are specific or unique to study samples whereas revalidation is a safeguard to ensure that obtained differentiations between more and less successful persons do not erode with the passage of time. To accomplish the necessary statistical analyses involved in the development, cross-validation and revalidation of empirically derived keys for scoring biodata items requires sizable numbers of study subjects and a level of technical expertise ordinarily available only to larger employers.

Peer ratings represent the other category of promising suitable alternatives. None of the studies reviewed by Reilly and Chao presented data pertaining specifically to the fairness of peer evaluations but the validity data are quite favorable: Average validities of .31, .51, and .37 were obtained against training, promotional, and job performance ratings criteria, respectively. Across all types of criteria, the average validity was .41. Reilly and Chao noted 2 drawbacks to the operational use of peer evaluations. First, peer ratings are rarely feasible for use in making hiring decisions since an employer ordinarily would not be able to obtain peer judgments about an applicant's job suitability. Second, where peer ratings are available and can be feasibly obtained, as in promotion situations, there are problems of standardization. A person working in a smaller group is more likely to receive a higher score than a person in a larger work unit. Differences in the size of the peer group present a measurement artifact that limits the usefulness of peer evaluations.

In summary, the review conducted by Reilly and Chao represents the most recent, comprehensive look at suitable alternatives to conventional employment tests. Of the 8 categories of alternative selection devices examined, only biodata and peer evaluations have track records that compare favorably with conventional employment tests in terms of validity, adverse impact, and fairness. But there are some problems associated with the use of biodata and peer evaluations.

RESEARCH ON EMPLOYMENT TESTS

This section summarizes the outcome of scholarly programmatic research in the area of employment tests. It seems fair to say that the passage of various equal employment regulations accelerated the pace of research activities and focused their direction. A sampling of the major findings is reviewed here. For convenience, the cumulative outcomes of these research endeavors is catalogued into 3 broad categories.

Research on Differential Validity and Test Fairness

The differential validity issue has to do with questions of whether a test that is valid for Group A (for example, blacks) also is valid and to the same extent as for Group B (for example, whites). The test fairness issue addresses the question of parity between the probability of "passing" the test and the probability of successful performance on the job. Together, questions of differential validity and test fairness converge on the broader question of whether test scores have the same meaning for different subgroups. On an even broader scale, the twin issues touch upon the more fundamental question of whether the same laws of behavior apply to blacks and whites, males and females, minorities and nonminorities.

The issue of differential validity is investigated by conducting a validation study separately for Group A and for Group B and comparing the resulting validity coefficients. Whether a test is fair or biased involves investigating the consequences of using test scores in the selection process. The research evidence accumulated to date is overwhelmingly in the direction that indicates that tests that are valid for 1 group are also valid for other groups and tests are fair predictors of job behavior in that the same level of qualifying test standards is associated with the same level of job performance for all examinees regardless of whether they are members of Group A or of Group B. The data thus confirm the commonsensical notion that if knowledge of mechanical principles is a bona fide requirement to competently perform the job, blacks, whites, males, and females will be required to possess the same level of mechanical knowledge if they are to attain the same level of job proficiency. Whatever lawful relationships are embodied in the correlation between test performance and job performance apply equally across race/sex lines.

Research on Validity Generalization

Are test validities transportable from 1 location or unit of a company to another location or unit? Or are test validities situation specific such that a validation study must be conducted in every nook and cranny where the employer intends to use the same tests to screen applicants for the same job?

These are questions illustrative of the questions that the research on validity generalization sought to answer.

The notion that validities might be situation specific arose out of the general finding that test validities tended to fluctuate from study to study. The wide variability in the outcome of validity studies involving the same job and the same test accounted for the early hypothesis that different factors were implicated in performing the same job from 1 study to the next. Later studies by F. Schmidt and his colleagues (Schmidt, Hunter, and Urry, 1976; Schmidt and Hunter, 1977; Schmidt, Hunter, Pearlman, and Shane, 1979) and by J. Callender and H. G. Osburn (1980) found that the same variability in obtained validity coefficients could be explained not by differences in underlying factor structures but by a number of statistical artifacts, such as sampling error, test and criterion unreliabilities, and restriction of range. These artifacts, which are present and operative under typical validation conditions, have the effect of lowering obtained validity coefficients, often to the point where the judgment is erroneously made that tests are not valid. The adjusted validity coefficients that emerge after corrections are made for the effects of various statistical artifacts justify the conclusion that tests are valid for more situations than previously supposed.

Research on the Practical Utility of Validated Tests

Research studies examining the economic impact of valid selection procedures are of fairly recent vintage. Although the theoretical formulations underlying the concept of test utility have been known for some time (Brogden, 1946; Cronbach and Gleser, 1965; Taylor and Russell, 1939), the application of various utility formulas for computing the gains associated with test use in the workplace has been hampered by the research community's inability to quantify test-related gains in dollar terms. As L. Cronbach and G. Gleser (1965) admit: "The assignment of values to outcomes is the Achilles' heel of decision theory" (p. 121).

F. Schmidt, J. Hunter, R. McKenzie, and T. Muldrow (1979) have recently devised an interesting methodology for estimating the dollar gains attributable to testing. The technique involves asking supervisors to estimate the dollar value of the output contributed by average employees and the corresponding output of low-performing and superior employees (for example, employees whose contribution falls 1 standard deviation on either side of the mean). By factoring in such items as the validity of the new procedure, the validity of the previous selection procedure, the cost of administering the new and the previous selection procedures, and the number of employees selected in a year, it becomes possible to compute the payoffs in dollars arising from using the new selection procedure. When this technique is applied to the selection of computer programmers, the estimated dollar gains are sizable. F. Schmidt and his colleagues estimated a productivity gain of close to $50 million from 1 year's use of a programmer test to select the 618 entry-level programmers for the federal government when the validity of the new programmer test is .76, the validity of the previous procedure is .20, and the top 20% of the test scorers are selected.

By way of summary, presented here is a digest of the major findings arising out of research studies that were conducted to provide data-based answers to questions that have been highlighted by the passage of antidiscrimination legislation. Because employment testing is embedded in a larger context involving cultural norms, social policies, and business practices, it is not surprising that the answers generated by the scientific community to the sorts of issues summarized in this section are of more than academic import. The hypothesis dealing with differential validity, for example, represents more than a provisional statement about a populational state of affairs that can be supported or refuted by collecting the appropriate empirical data. The answers will determine whether there is any scientific merit to the notion that tests behave differently for different subgroups. The scientific answers may, in turn, affect the thinking of federal administrative agencies toward the requirement that separate validation studies be conducted for different subgroups—a requirement that is likely to strain the resources of smaller organizations, driving them to the posture of abandoning the more objective conventional tests with their track record of validity in favor of subjective selection criteria that are presumed to be less likely to be audited but whose past record of validity is either unknown or known to be low. The choice of which selection procedures to use should be based on comparative merits rather than on mandated requirements that apply more harshly to some selection procedures than to others and that are founded on hypotheses that are no longer professionally tenable.

CAUTIOUS RETURN TO EMPLOYMENT TESTING

Surveys of test use have documented a decline in testing activity, at least in the private sector. Only 42% of the sample of personnel executives polled by BNA in 1976 reported giving tests to prospective employees; this is a drop from the 90% reported by BNA in a comparable survey conducted in 1963. Among respondents of the 1975 Prentice Hall/ASPA survey who use tests, 75% reported cutting down on their testing program during the past 5 years. The factors contributing to the decline in employment testing activity doubtless include what the Prentice Hall/ASPA survey called "equal employment opportunity pressures generally."

If there is a cautious return to employment testing, it will be due to the following factors:

(a) The emergence of 1 set of government testing guidelines. There have been a number of these guidelines issued since the passage of the 1964 Civil Rights Act. For a period of about 2 years (1976-1978), 2 sets of federal testing guidelines with nonidentical provisions were in existence: the so-called Federal Executive Agency or FEA guidelines that were issued by the then Civil Service Commission, the Department of Justice, and the Department of Labor, and the EEOC guidelines that were first published in 1970 and that the EEOC republished unchanged in 1976. While it is commendable that the responsible federal agencies charged with administering antidiscrimination regulations have attempted to keep pace with changes in the case law and with relevant research findings, test users are understandably frustrated and confused by the frequency of the changes and by inconsistencies between the FEA and the EEOC guidelines. The latter source of confusion was eliminated in September 1978 when the responsible federal agencies issued the *Uniform Guidelines on Employee Selection Procedures.* A uniform set of testing guidelines does not necessarily make the burden of compliance any lighter but a uniform set of ground rules certainly alleviates the burden of understanding what it is that a test user must comply with.

(b) Recognition by those who gave up testing in the wake of Title VII's passage and the subsequent case law that alternative selection procedures, such as the interview or reference checks, are also considered "tests" and are therefore equally covered by the antidiscrimination provisions of the law.

(c) Realization that there are probably no real alternatives to conventional tests when such factors as validity, adverse impact, fairness, operational feasibility, and cost effectiveness are considered. Reilly and Chao's (1982) review of the literature yielded 2 possible categories of alternative selection procedures—biodata and peer evaluations—but there are technical as well as practical problems associated with their operational use in the workplace.

(d) Appreciation of the outcome of programmatic research in the area of employment testing that showed that tests are equally valid for and fair to all groups; tests have greater generalizability across situations/settings than previously thought; and tests yield practical payoffs that can be quantified in dollar terms and these payoffs are in excess of what one might expect.

(e) Administrative advantages of conventional paper-and-pencil employment tests that include greater efficiency in that they can be administered to a group of examinees in 1 testing session; greater standardization in that tests can be administered and scored in an objective, uniform fashion; and minimal training requirements for test administrators. The administrative advantages associated with maintaining tests on-line, coupled with their track record of validity and the emerging findings pertaining to their generalizability and utility, give conventional employment tests the distinct edge over any alternative selection procedure.

THE CASE FOR EMPLOYMENT TESTING

This section has been written to provide a sort of status report on the state of employment testing today. It has been shown that the incidence of test use is quite high and that confidence is supported by findings reported by the scientific community to the effect that tests are valid and fair predictors of job performance whose use yields sizable practical payoffs. Moreover, there appear to be no real alternatives to conventional tests. The case for employment testing on purely technical grounds is fairly strong. But is there a catch somewhere? Stated differently, are there considerations other than the purely technical that must be weighed in the development and use of testing devices?

The last 2 decades have seen employment tests in the limelight of social controversy, legal debate, and scientific research inquiry. Tests have been placed squarely on center court by 2 apparently conflicting forces: the widespread use of employment testing devices to aid decision makers in selecting the right person for the right job—on which testing devices nonminorities score higher as a group than their minority counter- parts—and legislation aimed at providing equal employment opportunity to all groups and affirmative action for the benefit of the historically disadvantaged. It is not likely that employment testing will be removed from the eye of controversy any time soon. But developments over the last 20 years in the research, governmental, and business circles have provided us with quite a bit of data that have called attention to the changing character of employment testing. In today's contemporary world, an employment test is at once a measuring device for registering individual differences in job-relevant characteristics among job candidates, a personnel tool for making selection decisions in which some job applicants will be accepted and others rejected, and a potential legal exhibit in a Title VII lawsuit in which a test-failing plaintiff alleges that the test's adverse impact is illegally discriminatory and not justified by business necessity. After the developments of the last several years, it is no longer respectable to conceptualize a testing issue solely as a psychometric problem even though technical soundness is a threshold requirement for viable testing programs. Similarly, to perceive the affirmative action commitments of a business as a "numbers game" is to misperceive the relationship between people numbers and the numbers of profitability. A business that is poring over the numbers called for by Chapter 11 of the Bankruptcy Act is not in the best position to play any other numbers game. To give up tests because they register group differences in test performance is to invoke the old saw about killing the messenger that brings the bad news. In brief, the 1-factor- at-a-time approach to employment testing is probably passé.

The catch occurs when test users make decisions based solely on a test's technical properties or its adverse impact or its cost effectiveness as a personnel tool for managing applicant flow. The challenge is to harmonize the technical, legal, and business parameters of testing into a coherent program of human resource management. The case for employment testing is a case for a balanced, systemic view of the multiple opportunities and constraints that impinge on what was once a fairly straightforward undertaking requiring little more than a stopwatch, a batch of test papers, answer sheets, and a scoring template. This expanded view of employment testing is both timely and salutary.

VALIDATION CONCEPTS

What is the meaning of test validity? How does one go about validating a test? What are the psychometric or professional requirements of test validation and what is the manager/test user's "piece of the action" in the process of showing that a test is job related?

This section presents answers to the foregoing questions in a format that resembles a primer in that only the more fundamental principles are covered. Because the thrust of the book is to integrate both the professional and the applied aspects of test validation and test use, a conscious decision was made to blend the 2 points of view at each step of the discussion. For convenience, each section begins with an exposition of the technical material followed by their practical ramifications.

BASIC CONCEPT OF VALIDITY

The basic concept in test validation is the notion of job relatedness. A test is said to be valid if it measures skills and abilities related to the competent performance of the job such that those who do well on the test have a higher probability of successfully performing the job than their lower-scoring counterparts. The relationship between test performance and job performance is at the heart of the validity concept: Low test performance is associated with low job performance while high test scores are associated with higher performance levels on the job. The higher the validity of the test, the stronger is the relationship between test performance and job performance.

The rationale for validity lies in matching 2 sets of variable data: individual differences in qualifications among members of the job applicant population and differences among jobs in what is required for successful job performance. Applicants differ among themselves on dimensions that range from what is observable (such as weight, height, and other physical characteristics) to characteristics that selection devices attempt to capture (such as skill and ability levels or specific job experience). Jobs also differ among themselves. Some jobs are done "by the number," while others permit the incumbent maximum latitude in structuring his workaday world, while still others require the exertion of physical effort or the use of specialized tools. Differences in job requirements have implications for the sorts of characteristics that job holders must have in order to contribute to the employing organization's mission. The applicant who is qualified for Job X may not necessarily be qualified for Job Y. A validated test enables one to tell which applicants, among the many who are called, should be selected.

Practical considerations. A validated test provides test users and other decision makers with information about a job candidate's likely performance on the job based on his test performance. If a test is valid, it can be used as an instrument of prediction for forecasting how a person is going to do on the job before the person is hired or promoted into it. The payoffs associated with the early identification of which prospective employees will work out on the job are quite obvious. The advantages are driven home when one considers that, without effective front-end screens into the job, performance during training or on-the-job performance (more expensive than conventional employment tests) function as screening mechanisms.

Test users should be cautioned about the probabilistic nature of the outcomes of validation research. The predictions based on test scores are not perfect and there will be occasional misses—the test passer who "looks good on paper" but does not deliver on the job as well as the applicant, rejected for failing to pass the test, who would have been a competent job performer. These cases are the exceptions to the rule that tend to attract attention. The value of a validated test, however, lies not in its ability to identify the exceptions but in its ability to improve the batting average of decision makers in selecting those who will work out on the job over many selection decisions and in the long run.

An invalid test does no one any good. It becomes a source of irrelevant difficulty to the test taker since applicants who pass the test are no more likely to do well on the job than those whose test scores are low. It fulfills no legitimate business purpose since invalid information is not credible information. Furthermore, use of an invalid test buys one legal exposure to potential antidiscrimination lawsuits.

METHODS OF VALIDATION

There are 3 traditional methods of validation: content, construct, and criterion-related. Content validation involves showing that the test is a representative sample of important work behaviors, such as job tasks, work duties, or job knowledges and skills. Criterion-related validation involves a showing of a statistical relationship between test performance and job performance. There are 2 basic strategies for conducting a criterion-related validation study: the predictive method in which the test is administered to job applicants and those hired are followed up on the job and their test scores are correlated with a criterion measure of job performance and the concurrent method in which incumbent employees are tested and their test scores are correlated with their job performance. Construct validation involves showing that the test measures an underlying characteristic or trait, such as "leadership" or "dominance," and that the trait in question is involved in the performance of the job to a significant degree. Construct validation has been likened to theory building in that it requires a comprehensive research program to develop the cumulative evidence necessary to support the hypothesis that the particular construct, although unobservable, underlies and gives coherence to test and nontest behavior.

Practical considerations. Content valid tests have a direct and discernible relationship with the job to which it is geared. This is because the test is frequently a miniature replica of aspects of the job. A typing test for clerical positions, for example, is valid by virtue of its content since performance on the test translates directly into performance of an important aspect of the job. The test resembles the job to a high degree. Content valid tests are said to possess a high degree of face validity since they appear valid to the nontechnical person.

Construct validation is more than a 1-shot study. It is a fairly elaborate strategy for demonstrating job relatedness and may involve a combination of content and criterion-related validation strategies. It is not surprising that construct validation is seldom used in employment selection research.

The parity among the 3 methods of validation is now widely recognized. The 1970 version of the EEOC guidelines on testing preferred criterion-related validation over content and construct validation, accepting the last 2 substitutes only when a criterion-related study was not technically feasible. The Supreme Court, in its *Washington v. Davis* decision (12 FEP 1415 (1976)), endorsed the professional view that each method was equally acceptable under the proper circumstances—a point of view adopted by the *Uniform Guidelines on Employee Selection Procedures.*

STEPS IN VALIDATION PROCESS

The major steps in conducting a criterion-related validation study are discussed below. The reader may wonder about the relevance of these steps to content and construct validation. It will be recalled that a number of studies, including a combination of content and criterion-related validity efforts, may be required to support the validity of a particular construct in the workplace. It is thus likely that criterion-related validity data will be part of the evidence making up a showing of a test's construct validity. With respect to content validity, the process of showing that the test representatively samples important aspects of the job involves, beyond the job analysis step, the exercise of professional judgment and expert opinion. Even after it is established that a test is valid by virtue of its content, however, it is still necessary to develop reasonable cutoff scores or qualifying standards for use by the employment office. Most frequently, the cutoff score is also established by means of expert judgment. A miniature criterion-related validation study, perhaps involving fewer study subjects than is ordinarily required, may be used to develop empirically based cutoff scores. The validation steps listed below would then be followed. Thus, the discussion to follow applies, in varying degrees, to each of the 3 traditional methods of test validation.

Practical considerations. Conducting a validation study in the workplace represents more than an aseptic scientific exercise in collecting data for testing hypotheses about the relationship between test performance and job performance. It is also an intrusion into the day-to-day operations of the enterprise and an identifiable organizational event that may raise implicit and exaggerated expectations that the outcome of the validity study would "fix" all sorts of organizational problems, including those that are beyond the reach of a sound testing program.

For organizations using paper-and-pencil testing devices for the first time, validation may be perceived as the prelude to the abdication of managerial flexibility and discretion in favor of rigid decision rules—a prospect that line management may find both threatening and distasteful. To pull off successfully a validation study requires that the technical as well as the organizational and logistical requirements be competently managed.

Job Analysis

Job analysis refers to the systematic study of job content and job context for the purpose of obtaining what the *Uniform Guidelines on Employee Selection Procedures* calls "a detailed statement of work behaviors and other information relevant to the job" (Sec. 16 (K)). Job analysis is a logical first step in the development of various personnel subsystems, such as training, job evaluation and test validation. In the area of training, for example, job analysis seeks to identify performance dimensions that can be enhanced by further training or deficiencies in need of remediation. In the area of job evaluation, where the focus is on determining the relative worth of different jobs for compensation purposes, job analysis yields the description of work content, which is then quantified to produce between-job comparisons on such compensable factors as skill, effort, responsibility, and working conditions. In test validation, the purpose of job analysis is twofold: to identify those organizationally significant aspects of the job that will serve as the criteria of job performance to be "predicted" by the tests and to identify the appropriate selection devices or tests (tests that measure the skills, abilities, and worker characteristics presumptively related to the criterion measures) that will make up the experimental or trial test battery.

Job analysis can be performed using a variety of methodological procedures, which include on-site observation of the work; interviews with job holders, their supervisors, or job experts; use of work diaries in which job holders maintain a running account of job activities; reference to such source documents as technical publications, training manuals, or existing job descriptions; and the critical incidents technique, which identifies specific job behaviors that are particularly effective or ineffective in attaining the job's mission. The procedures are not mutually exclusive. A combination of techniques frequently yields the desired job information. The present author prefers developing job information based upon interviews with subject matter experts—the incumbents who are knowledgeable about the job because they perform it and first-level supervisors who are accountable for getting the job done—supplemented by a visit to the workplace.

Practical considerations. Job analysis represents the first interface between the line organization and the researcher. It sets the tone for the rest of the study activities: The more smoothly the job analysis portion goes, the better for all concerned. Technical competency, shown by a disciplined approach to the collection of relevant job information rather than trivial or fascinating "gee whiz" information, coupled with due concern for the departments contributing interviewees to the job analysis process, will go a long way in ensuring that the study gets off to the right start.

Job analysis is the cornerstone to the development of a number of personnel subsystems. Ideally, then, the job description developed for test validation purposes should be suitable for job evaluation purposes and vice versa. This ideal will continue to be an elusive goal for as long as job analysts can do no better than write job descriptions consisting of what may be called "universal task statements." Universal task statements are tasks that are characteristic of most jobs yet distinguish between none of them. A few such tasks are shown below.

1. Establish priority for the day's work.
2. Follow prescribed practices in meeting company objectives.
3. Show courtesy and tact in dealings with customers.
4. Refer unusual or emergency situations to supervisor.
5. Repeat the same operations many times in the day.
6. Cover for employees who are on vacation.
7. Use judgment in resolving problems not previously encountered.
8. Maintain record of work completed.
9. Attend company-sponsored training to maintain and enhance skill level.
10. Perform other duties as required.

Development of Criterion Measures of Job Performance

Most textbooks in personnel selection consider criterion development as the most important step in the validation process, and with good reason since criterion measures should represent those aspects of worker behavior that are relevant to the organization's mission and that validated tests seek to predict. In an ideal world, it should be possible to develop an index of a worker's overall worth to the employing organization—an index that registers the person's total contribution to the attainment of corporate objectives. This index would represent the ultimate criterion and tests that predict a prospective employee's standing on the ultimate criterion would be worth their weight in gold. In the real world, proxy measures of job performance are used to make judgments about the effectiveness of testing devices and prediction systems.

The types of criterion measures employed in validation studies include production data (for example, quantity and quality of output), personnel data (for example, absences, turnover, rate of advancement), and supervisory evaluations in the form of rankings or ratings. Supervisory ratings represent the most frequently used criterion, largely because they are fairly easy to obtain.

The choice of which criterion measure to use in a given validation study is left up to the professional judgment of the investigator. The following considerations are important guidelines in selecting and developing criterion measures:

1. Criterion measures should represent important aspects of the job. There is very little point in predicting criteria that are trivial. In the words of the *Uniform Guidelines*: "These measures or criteria are relevant to the extent that they represent critical or important job duties, work behaviors or work outcomes as developed from the review of job information." (Sec. 14B[2])
2. Performance on the criterion measure should reflect individual differences in the ability to perform the job rather than differences in work assignments, group

size, nature of supervision, and other variables that are beyond the control of the worker.

3. Criterion measures should be psychometrically sound: The criterion information should be collected in as standardized a fashion as possible and it should include enough observations to be reliable as well as allow for a meaningful spread of scores in order to accommodate differentiations among study subjects.

4. Collection of the criterion information must be administratively feasible. This is a practical consideration that becomes more important the longer the data collection period with the necessary intrusion of validation research requirements into the day-to-day operations of the workplace.

Practical considerations. When supervisory evaluations are used as criterion measures of job performance—as they are in most validation studies—there are 2 phenomena that management should be aware of: rater tendencies and criterion contamination.

Rater tendencies refer to tendencies by supervisors to displace their evaluations to certain portions of the rating scale. The 3 most common rater tendencies are best illustrated with a hypothetical rating form. Assume that the criterion measure consists of supervisory evaluations of 4 performance dimensions (for example, job knowledge, work execution, interpersonal relationships, overall effectiveness) and that a 7-point rating scale is used to rate study subjects on each dimension. Halo is the rater tendency that characterizes the supervisor who rates a person about the same way on the 4 performance dimensions because of an overall general impression. Central tendency characterizes the supervisor who avoids the high or low ends of the scale by giving out mostly average ratings. Most of the ratings would cluster around the center of the scale, with numerical values between 3 and 5. Leniency is the tendency to displace one's ratings toward either the favorable or the unfavorable portion of the rating scale. Skewed ratings (mostly 1s and 2s or 6s and 7s) are the telltale signs of leniency. Rater tendencies have the effect of restricting the range of differentiations among study subjects, thereby lowering the apparent validity of the test. Clearer definition of the performance dimensions on which study subjects will be evaluated, use of behavioral examples to illustrate what different points on the rating scale mean, and training of supervisors on the use of the rating form are practical steps that can be taken to minimize rater tendencies.

Criterion contamination occurs when supervisors gain access to the test scores of their subordinates and this knowledge influences how they subsequently rate their subordinates' job performance. Criterion contamination resembles a self-fulfilling prophecy and has the effect of inflating the obtained validity coefficient; it can be avoided by filing away the study subjects' test papers unscored until such time as the criterion measures are obtained and the investigator is ready to run the correlation between test performance and supervisory ratings of job performance.

Selection of Predictors

"Predictor" is the generic name given for a selection device that is validated for the purpose of determining whether the skill, ability, or worker characteristic being measured by the selection device is correlated with performance on the criterion. Conventional tests, job interviews, and reference checks are examples of predictors that are used in the employment context to predict job behavior. In the first section, 8 different categories of predictors were described that R. R. Reilly and G. Chao (1982) examined in a review of possible alternatives to conventional paper-and-pencil tests. For the 2 categories that were found to be promising (biodata and peer evaluations), the technical and operational requirements involved in implementing them were summarized.

It is beyond the scope of this book to present a review of different tests that are available to an organization that is contemplating the use of testing devices for employment purposes. For most tests, a review by experts in the testing field can be found in 1 of the several issues of *Mental Measurement Yearbooks*. Another publication, *Tests in Print*, provides a comprehensive listing of most available tests.

Practical considerations. Selection devices can be classified into 1 of 2 broad categories: ability and skill measures, which indicate whether the examinee can do the job, and more motivational measures, which indicate whether the person will do the job. The ideal selection battery consists of a combination of can do and will do measures to capture the nonoverlapping determinants of successful job performance. Paper-and-pencil tests are best suited for measuring the "can do" dimensions; the interview can be structured to measure the more motivational correlates of job behavior as these may be discernible from such indicators as the applicant's past employment history, work habits, and interest patterns.

It is customary, when conducting a validation study, to include more tests in the experimental battery than one expects to use operationally in order to increase the odds of coming up with a valid set of tests at the conclusion of the criterion-related validity effort. Even if all the tests in the trial battery are subsequently shown to be valid, however, it may not be feasible to use them all operationally. Practical constraints having to do with the cost of testing and the length of the testing session as well as technical considerations having to do with reaching a point of diminishing returns in prediction (beyond some optimum number of tests, little gain is realized by adding more tests to the battery) place an upper limit to the number of tests that are adopted for operational use.

Tests are available from commercial publishers. The developmental costs involved in producing a test that meets psychometric and professionally acceptable specifications can be hefty. The typical test user could more profitably divert the expenditure to a validation study aimed at determining which tests will work for his specific situation. If the test publisher is reputable, tests selected off the shelf should be good; the test user's piece of the action is to determine what the tests are good for (that is, perform a validation study).

Development of Study Sample

Study samples in a criterion-related validation study refer to those persons who will be administered the experimental battery of tests and whose on-the-job performance will be used as criterion measures. It will be recalled that there are 2 basic designs for performing a validation study. In the concurrent method, incumbent employees in the job for which the test is being validated are used as study subjects, while in the predictive method, tests are administered to job candidates before they are hired into the job in question. Each method has its own advantages and disadvantages. The concurrent method has been faulted for using persons as study subjects who may not be representative of the applicant population to which the prediction system will be applied. Incumbents, for example, may not be motivated to do well on the tests since their test performance will not affect their entry into a job they already hold. On the criterion side, present employees may not be representative to the extent that more able peers will presumably have been promoted out of the job and unsuccessful ones will have been terminated. But the big advantage to the present employee or concurrent method is the ready availability of study subjects, making it possible to expedite the end-to-end conduct of the study. The obverse is true for the predictive model. The use of job applicants in the predictive design resembles the actual employment situation in their mental set to do well on the test and yields a sample whose criterion performance is less restricted in range. The drawback lies in the length of time it may take to generate the desired number of study subjects. When intake of prospective employees into the job is slow, a predictive design may not be advisable.

There are 2 conditions that may render a criterion-related study of either the predictive or the concurrent variety technically infeasible. One constraint has to do with severe restriction of range on either the predictor or the criterion variable. If only the top 10% of the test scorers or the top 10% of the job performers are available for the study, there is hardly any variability available to be predicted. The other conditions deals with sample size. Until recently, a rule of thumb dictated that a validation study was not feasible unless one had at least 30 study subjects. The thinking now is that this lower limit of 30 is on the low side. Thus, adequate variability in predictor and criterion scores as well as adequate sample size are threshold requirements for a criterion-related validation study.

Practical considerations. It should be fairly obvious that a usable study subject is one with scores on the test and the criterion of job performance. It is advisable to wait for some reasonable period after the person is placed on the job before criterion measurements are obtained in order to allow the person's performance to stabilize and get over the first-day-at-work syndrome. If the waiting period is too long, turnover may take its toll. If the turnover is differential in that either the better or the poorer employees tend to leave, restriction of range will compound the problem of study subject loss. On the other hand, if turnover is used as the criterion and turnover is low, one may have to wait a very long time to complete the study.

The *Uniform Guidelines* calls for "studies of test fairness whenever technically feasible" (Section 14 B(8)). This provision is tantamount to a requirement to perform separate validity studies for different race/sex groups in order to generate the necessary data for the statistical comparisons. This provision is at variance with the research evidence that indicates that tests have the same meaning for different subgroups.

Discussed above is the need for a broad range of scores on both the predictor and the criterion variables as 1 pre-condition to the feasibility of a criterion-related validity study. Ensuring a broad range of scores on the predictor side translates into a requirement to hire low-scoring applicants. Understandably, management will not embrace this prospect with enthusiasm. There are 2 ways of handling this situation. One is to lock up the test booklets unscored and let the nontest modules of the employment process perform the screening function during the period of time that the tests are being validated. Another way of meeting the requirement is to involve more units of the organization in the validation study and to assign quotas of low test scorers to the participating units, thereby spreading the load around.

Statistical Analyses

The discipline of statistics plays 3 generic roles in a criterion-related validation study. One is to summarize the data for ease of understanding. The relationship between test scores and criterion scores, for example, is conveniently expressed by the correlation coefficient—a single number that summarizes the extent to which performance on the test is associated with performance on the job. Similarly, the distribution of predictor and criterion scores can be captured by computing the mean and the standard deviation. The second function of statistics is inferential in nature and has to do with evaluating whether obtained results are statistically significant or whether they can be attributed to chance. If a predictor-criterion correlation of .35 is obtained on a sample of 50 study subjects, for example, inferential statistics provide the ground rules for determining whether a result as high or higher than that obtained reflects a true validity state of affairs in the population or whether the result could be due to sampling fluctuations. The third function of statistics is to assemble the optimal battery of tests for operational use. The interest here is in determining which tests are to be used in combination and how each test is to be weighted.

Practical considerations. Data crunching has been aided greatly by high-speed computer technology. Statistical calculations that used to take hours to do by hand now take milliseconds of computer time. The practitioner's piece of the action is to ensure that the data input are accurate and that the outcomes of statistical analyses are interpreted in ways that do not offend common sense.

Test validities, usually expressed in terms of correlation coefficients, can be represented graphically by means of expectancy tables or expectancy charts. These tables show, at various score levels on the test, the proportion of selectees who can be expected to be successful on the job. See *Q-59* for illustrative samples of hypothetical expectancy charts.

Implementation of Study Results

Conducting a validation study is an undertaking that calls for the expertise of the researcher, the predictor and criterion scores of study subjects, the cooperation of line management, and funding by the sponsoring client department. Planning for the study should consider the technical as well as the administrative aspects and should include strategies for implementing study results.

Practical considerations. Using the validated test battery for the right job is an end-of-study issue that is best addressed when first planning for the study. The issue looms large in organizations where employees holding the same job title may be performing different work functions or where employees performing similar tasks may be holding different job titles. Where the validated test battery is to be used for higher than entry-level jobs on the basis of the so-called flow-through concept, collecting the supporting data pertaining to employee mobility and progression structures could be started even while the study is in progress. In short, one does not have to wait till the end of the study to start planning for how to utilize the products of selection research. While it is true that implementation strategies involve largely administrative considerations, the insights of the investigator could prove useful. The transition from research to implementation would then involve more than a ritualistic scenario in which the investigator goes off to do his thing and then hands off a technical report to the sponsoring department.

Most organizations process job candidates on a more or less regular basis and at a rate that is dictated by economic conditions and internal growth projections. It is thus not unusual for the employment office to build up a pending file of qualified applicants awaiting placement as vacancies occur. These applicants would be considered qualified under the old employment criteria where the old employment standards do not include performance on the test battery now being put on line. At cutover to the newly validated test battery, the test user could require applicants in the pending placement file to pass the new selection criteria or they could be grandfathered on the basis of the "once qualified, always qualified" rationale. There are undoubtedly other strategies for handling this situation. This discussion is not intended to exhaust the possibilities but to point to the importance of incorporating implementation issues into the planning of a validation study. One practical way to address this particular implementation issue is to avoid building up a backlog of applicants qualified under the old employment standards that need special treatment at cutover to the newly validated test battery.

Following cutover and on a long-term basis, the implementation concern centers on measures for safeguarding and maintaining the security of testing devices. The validity of a testing program remains viable only for as long as test scores continue to reflect individual differences in underlying skills and abilities, not differential access to test booklets or scoring keys.

COST OF VALIDATION STUDIES

This section concludes by considering what it costs to conduct a validation study. The 1975 Prentice-Hall/ASPA survey shows a fairly wide range, from under $5,000 (reported by 71.6% of those respondents who have conducted validation) to more than $20,000 (reported by 3.1% of the respondents). Not unexpectedly, larger companies reported spending more money than their smaller counterparts. It is clear that validation represents a fairly substantial economic investment on the part of the test user. Cost factors were cited as 1 of the 8 validation headaches in the same survey. Where it is technically feasible to do so, it seems that validation is a worthwhile investment.

Are there steps that can be taken to make the validation process more cost-effective, perhaps by maximizing the benefits from the study outcomes or by minimizing some of the cost items? The Prentice-Hall/ASPA survey suggests that consortium or joint validation studies with other organizations are a possibility. Interest in consortium studies was high among survey respondents, ranging from 60% among respondents with 100 to 499 employees to 20% among respondents with more than 25,000 employees. The appeal of joint validation efforts is twofold: The resulting pooled sample size permits a criterion-related study to be performed where it would otherwise not be technically feasible because of inadequate number of study subjects and the consortium approach spreads the costs across the participating organizations.

The judicious and effective use of consultants can give organizations without the in-house technical expertise the capability of performing a validation study. In order to use consultant services effectively, the test user should delineate, in fairly specific terms, what aspects of the study can be done with in-house resources and what aspects can appropriately be farmed out. The more clearly the consultant's role is defined and the more definitively the work products and the schedule for delivery can be buttoned down, the better for all concerned. The author's personal experience indicates that eliminating the element of surprise in advance of signing the contract effectively reduces misunderstandings and ill feelings several months and several thousand dollars later.

Maximizing the benefits from the outcome or by-product of the validity effort is another way of getting the most mileage from one's research dollars. To illustrate, in a previous section, it was indicated that job analysis is a major component in the development of a number of personnel subsystems, such as training, performance appraisal, job evaluation, and test validation. It is possible to describe jobs in terms that will be suitable not only for test validation purposes but for training and job evaluation purposes as well. The manager may challenge his consultant performing job analysis in conjunction with a validity study to come up with work products that will also be suitable for other human resource applications. A job description that meets the needs of multiple users is not only a cost-effective measure but is indicative of a disciplined approach to the management of dollar and human resources,

To conclude, a recurring sentiment is echoed. What is true for employment testing holds true for validation: Neither one should be regarded as an incidental, stand-alone project in a milieu of organizational happenings; both activities are best understood as integral components in a decision maker's program for managing the human resources of the enterprise.

Part I
EMPLOYMENT TESTING— THE BUSINESS CONTEXT

Q-1 How are tests used in the employment process?

The employment process is essentially a process of selecting the right person for the job, that is, determining the degree of fit between job requirements and the skills, abilities, and characteristics of job candidates. Employment tests, where they are used, are designed principally to aid in matching job requirements with applicant characteristics. In addition, tests fulfill the administrative function of managing the flow of job candidates to the more expensive modules of the employment process. (See *Q-6* for the other steps in the employment process.)

Q-2 What is a selection problem?

A selection problem is one in which many are called but few are chosen. The most obvious example might be one where there is 1 job vacancy and 10 applicants express the desire to fill it. Similarly, when technological innovations displace a fraction of the work force, the decision to terminate workers in reverse order of their seniority is also a selection problem for which the seniority clauses in some union contracts provide the answer.

The number of openings relative to the number of applicants, called the selection ratio, is an important concept with implications for the usefulness of a selection procedure. To illustrate, if the selection ratio is 1.0 indicating that there are only as many applicants as there are openings, the employer does not have a selection problem. He is "stuck" with the applicants that the poor labor market conditions give him and no test or selection procedure, however high its validity, will help him. Testing, in situations where the selection ratio is 1.0, is a superfluous and irrelevant enterprise from the point of view of enhancing the quality of the hires. However, as the selection ratio improves and the employer can afford to be more selective, a test of modest validity can help the employer "skim the cream" in order to identify prospective workers with the highest probability of successfully performing the job.

All of the foregoing is another way of saying that, in order for a test to "work" in selecting the best qualified, it must be given the opportunity to make the appropriate selections.

Q-3   What is the psychological rationale underlying selection systems?

Selecting the right person for the job is a shorthand way of expressing the objective of employment decisions. To elaborate, jobs differ—they differ in the sorts of activities and behaviors that are required to successfully perform them. Some jobs are cyclical and repetitive, involving operations that are done "by the number," while others are less structured, allowing the incumbent greater discretion in the choice of procedures and methods. Some require the use of tools or the operation of machines; still others are highly abstract, calling for the exercise of cognitive skills. In short, jobs differ in their requirements and these differences, in turn, are reflected in the kinds and levels of abilities, skills, and worker characteristics required of incumbents. Selection systems are designed to identify worker characteristics, measurable by tests and other assessment procedures, that are related to job requirements.

The employment process is a process of progressively refining the degree of fit between characteristics of prospective job incumbents and job requirements. The different components of the employment process should ideally yield nonoverlapping measurements of job relevant characteristics. Paper-and-pencil tests, for example, are best suited to tapping the more cognitive aspects of the job while the interview measures the more motivational or interpersonal determinants of job performance. To the extent that the different components of the selection process measure unique (that is, nonoverlapping) job-related characteristics, to that extent will their use in combination enhance the prediction of job behavior.

Q-4 Does not an employment test's function of screening out unqualified applicants confirm the popular belief that tests are powerful gatekeepers to employment opportunities?

The observation that some applicants survive the employment process and become employed while others are disqualified by virtue of failing to meet test standards does highlight the screening function of employment tests and may contribute to unfavorable impressions about tests in general. On the other hand, the fact that some make it while others do not on the testing module of the employment process is the natural consequence of setting test standards and of acting on those standards operationally to arrive at accept/reject decisions. The more relevant and substantive questions are those that pertain to whether the test in question measures job-relevant characteristics (that is, whether the test has been validated) and whether the cutoff score is reasonable and consistent with the needs of the business. Both the validation and the cutoff score questions are technical in nature to which is added the consideration that has to do with managing the human resources requirements of the business by integrating the objectives of affirmative action programs with known group differences in the human condition.

Q-5 Does every employing organization use tests in the employment process?

No. Not every employer uses employment tests nor is it necessary for every employer to have a testing program. However, every organization that is faced with a selection problem in which there are more applicants for the limited number of available openings must develop its own strategy for deciding who gets rejected and who is accepted.

We recognize that an employer who accepts some applicants in favor of others makes an employment decision and the basis for that decision (such as interviews, reference checks, and the like) is included in the expansive definition of "tests" in the *Uniform Guidelines on Employee Selection Procedures*. See *Q-99*, Part 3. As pointed out in the first section, the term "test" is used to refer to the traditional paper-and-pencil devices that are historically used to assess job qualifications. Limiting the definition of tests to these sorts of instruments, this answer asserts that it is not feasible for every employer to have a test in his arsenal of selection procedures in order to properly evaluate job qualifications. Employment decisions can be made—accurately and responsibly—without the use of employment tests.

Q-6 What other steps are involved in the employment process?

Listed below are the major modules that comprise the typical employment process together with a few comments and the generic functions served by each module:

Application blank. The application blank is frequently the first paper record that documents the transaction between employer and potential employees. Despite variations between employing organizations, the core information elicited by the typical application blank can be grouped into the following categories: identifying information, work history, military service, specific work experience or skills, educational or training attainment, and personal or work references. Recent governmental regulations have imposed restrictions on the sorts of information that may be elicited by the application blank. For example, questions pertaining to the applicant's race, sex, age, religion, marital status, and arrest record may not be asked.

The generic functions of the application blank include:

- providing a record of employment activity that may be useful for internal purposes (for example, for monitoring the effects of affirmative recruiting efforts) as well as for compiling adverse impact statistics;
- providing demographic information about prospective employees for payroll and other administrative purposes;
- providing background data about the applicant's work history, educational attainment and specific skills for use as leads or clues in planning the selection interview.

Job interview. The interview is probably the most frequently and universally used selection procedure. The distinction is sometimes made between the screening or preliminary interview (where the primary interest is in identifying gross disqualifiers such as inability to work the hours and days required by the job or unsatisfactory motor vehicle driving record or alien status restrictions) and the evaluation interview (in which the interviewer takes a comprehensive, in-depth look at characteristics of the prospective employee-interviewee).

The evaluation and the preliminary interview serve the following generic functions in the employment process:

- as a public relations tool, the interview provides the opportunity for a representative of the company, in a 2-way, face-to-face dialogue, to promote the company's image to the labor market from which the company hopes to attract qualified personnel;
- as a selection device, the interview develops information about the applicant that can be used to predict the likelihood of his successful job performance.

The interview has been the object of a number of research studies. See *Q–8* for a synopsis of the outcomes.

Employment testing. As indicated in *Q–5*, not every organization uses tests as part of the employment process; those that do use tests primarily as a fairly efficient and standardized way of screening for job-relevant standards and, secondarily, as a way of managing the flow of job candidates to the more expensive modules of the employment process.

Reference checks. This category includes reference reports, letters of recommendation, work reference checks, and the like that are used to obtain information about the applicant from sources (for example, previous employers, teachers, coworkers, and relatives or acquaintances) presumably familiar with the applicant's background or work.

Reference checks serve two generic purposes:

- they are used to verify the information provided in the application blank;
- they provide information for predicting the probable job performance of the applicant.

The usefulness of the information developed in any module of the employment process depends on the accuracy of that information. Several factors, unique to reference checks vis-à-vis the other pre-employment modules, adversely affect the usefulness of the information developed from reference checks:

(a) Pre-selection: "Everyone has at least two good friends who will vouch for them" speaks to the problem that occurs when applicants select the persons who will provide testimonials about their background.

(b) Undifferentiated narratives: Reference reports that say the same things about all applicants or that say only good things about them are not likely to provide the sort of information that will be useful in differentiating between applicants. This is an example of the *restriction of range* problem (discussed more fully in *Q-46*), which has the effect of depressing validity. The tendency to write glittering generalizations and to highlight the applicant's strong points selectively while overlooking or glossing over his areas of weakness limit the usefulness of reference checks as predictors of subsequent job behavior. Legal considerations such as those that have to do with potential disclosure of reference narratives under the Freedom of Information Act or with the need to protect an individual's rights to privacy would tend to reinforce the tendency toward predominantly positive reference reports.

(c) Validity evidence: The research evidence bearing on the validity of reference reports for predicting job success is sparse. The few studies that exist do not paint an encouraging picture of validity for this particular module of the employment process—for reasons that are not surprising in light of the pre-selection and restriction of range phenomena cited above.

Medical evaluation. The last step in the employment process is typically some sort of medical evaluation aimed at determining whether the applicant is "fit for duty." The information developed in the medical portion of the employment process may be used to identify handicapped applicants and to determine whether the handicapping condition can be reasonably accommodated in the workplace.

The discussion of the employment process looked at both the administrative and the predictive (as a selection device) aspects of each module. The use of tests to manage the flow of applicants to the other modules of the employment process, on the one hand, and to identify from among many applicants those who are most likely to succeed on the job, on the other hand, illustrates the administrative and the predictive aspects, respectively. Sequencing of the modules is largely a matter of managerial discretion, taking into account the relative costs of each module and the optimal scheduling of applicants to be processed by existing staff. Each step is a winnowing process in which the match between job requirements and applicant characteristics is progressively refined.

With respect to the selection function of the different modules, 2 concluding observations are relevant. First, the different components of the employment process should ideally yield nonoverlapping measurements of job-relevant characteristics. Paper-and-pencil tests, for example, are used to tap the more cognitive aspects of the job (sometimes referred to as the "can do" correlates of job behavior), while the interview measures the more motivational (the "will do") determinants of job performance. To the extent that the different components measure different or nonoverlapping job-related characteristics, to that extent will their use in combination enhance the prediction of job behavior.

The second consideration recognizes that the expansive definition of "tests" in the *Uniform Guidelines on Employee Selection Procedures* applies to each module of the employment process. Bottom-line statistics, the 4/5ths rule of thumb, adverse impact, and job relatedness are concepts applicable to all the modules and not limited to the paper-and-pencil tests.

Q-7 Does every applicant go through the entire employment process?

There are 2 generic circumstances under which applicants may not be processed from beginning to end: when they are disqualified along the way or when the company has built up a bank of qualified candidates in its pending placement files to accommodate anticipated personnel requisitions.

Q-8 What sorts of studies have been conducted on the interview?

The interview has been studied from several points of view. For convenience, the studies have been clustered into generic categories and the major outcomes of the studies are discussed within each category.

Interviewing process. Studies of the dynamics involved in the decision-making process as it occurs in the interview have yielded the following findings:

- Interviews that are patterned or structured provide higher interrater reliability or agreement than unstructured interviews. The structured interview enhances the reliability of the process by increasing the consistency of what is covered and by facilitating standardization of how bits of information are to be interpreted or weighted.
- Interviewers tend to overreact to negative information and are influenced more by unfavorable than by favorable information about the applicant.
- Interviewers make up their minds early about the interviewee's suitability, with the decision taking place during the first half of the interview.
- Interviewers tend to talk more than the interviewees—a finding that goes counter to the fact-finding role of the interview.

Interviewing outcomes. Here the focus is on the interview as a selection device and on the psychometric properties (notably, reliability, and validity) of the interviewer judgments/decisions.

- As noted above, structuring the interview enhances its reliability by standardizing what information is collected and how the information is to be evaluated.
- The validity evidence for the interview is not impressive: the record of validity is low and, when interviews are used in combination with valid test data, the validity of the resulting composite is generally not appreciably higher than the validity for test scores alone.
- Of the characteristics that have been studied, the cognitive traits of intelligence or mental ability are most reliably measured by the interview. Paper-and-pencil tests measure the same traits more reliably and more efficiently.

The interview is the most widely used selection procedure. The richness of the information that can be elicited and its flexibility for assessing different applicant characteristics are 2 reasons for the popularity of this selection device. The seemingly universal urge to see a prospective employee "in the flesh" is another reason. Studies of the interview reveal that the richness of the information generated can be a double-edged sword that cuts both ways. The information stream may become so varied that standardization (in terms of what areas are covered and how the bits of information are to be weighted) becomes a problem. The dynamics of the interviewing process (where the interviewer tends to make up his mind early based on an uneven consideration of favorable and unfavorable information about the interviewee) affect the outcomes of the interview as a selection device. These outcomes, which are psychometric in nature, have to do with reliability and validity considerations: The information generated by the job interview has to be relevant (that is, valid) and reliable in that 2 or more interviewers are able to agree on their assessment of the same applicant.

The technical considerations pertaining to standardization, reliability, and validity are not unique to the job interview; they apply to all selection procedures. However, unlike more objective paper-and-pencil selection devices such as tests, the subjective nature of the interview renders it additionally vulnerable to criticisms peculiar to subjective evaluation systems. These criticisms have to do with the vague and amorphous nature of the criteria for job suitability and with the controlling weight given to interviewer decisions in the hiring process—two factors that render the interview "a ready mechanism for invidious discrimination" against minority applicants.

This discussion is concluded by pointing out that in addition to empirical studies on the interview, there are "how to" books that focus on interviewing techniques. Pointers on how to set the stage, alleviate interviewee anxiety, capitalize on pauses and similar admonitions on interviewing style are frequently combined with recommendations for the training of interviewers, development of explicit standards for assessing job suitability and thorough coverage of the applicant's background—practices that are likely to increase the standardization and reliability of the interview, thereby enhancing its psychometric quality as a selection device. That is to say, if the problems are correlated (lack of standardization leads to low reliability which in turn reduces validity), the "fixes" tend to bring about correlated benefits.

Q–9   Why do employment tests focus on the abilities rather than on the personality or motivational characteristics of the applicant?

Tests of mental ability have been around much longer than measures of personality or motivation. Mental ability testing dates back to 1905 when S. Binet developed the first intelligence test to identify the quick from the slow learners among school children. The first intelligence test was individually administered, calling for a 1-on-1 transaction between examinee and test administrator. Subsequently, mental ability tests were used on a massive scale during the period of rapid mobilization brought about by World War II when group-administered tests were given to thousands of recruits. If tests could be used to process recruits for various military assignments, why couldn't they be used for screening job applicants? The transition from the military setting to the industrial workplace was not difficult to make.

The reasons for the greater usage of mental ability tests relative to more motivational measures go beyond the historical accident of being on the scene first. Two generic reasons account for the greater popularity of mental ability tests.

ADMINISTRATIVE

As a general rule, mental ability tests are more efficient than tests of personality or motivation in providing information about applicant characteristics. Typically, mental ability tests are relatively short, group-administered tests in which examinees record their responses on machine-scorable answer sheets. The scoring and interpretation are generally straightforward, often requiring no more than superimposing a scoring template on the examinee's answer sheet, counting off the number of correct answers, and referring to a chart to determine whether the total score meets the established cutoff score. The assessment of personality or motivational characteristics, on the other hand, calls for more elaborate procedures to administer, score, and interpret. It is not unusual for personality tests to be administered on an individual basis. Proper interpretation of examinee responses generally requires specialized training. Even when tests of personality or motivation are presented in paper-and-pencil format so that they are suitable for group administration, development of the "correct" or keyed answers entails fairly sophisticated research studies. The seemingly mundane task of giving examinees feedback on their test performance becomes a more involved undertaking with personality or motivational measures than with ability tests. Finally, personality or motivational inventories are subject to charges of containing items that are offensive, border on invading one's privacy or are otherwise in poor taste. In sum, there are procedural advantages with using mental ability tests and these advantages translate into administrative efficiency that becomes significant as the number of job applicants to be tested increases.

PSYCHOMETRIC

Tests of personality or motivation are subject to a number of test-taking tendencies and response biases that operate to distort the scores obtained. One such tendency is to answer in the direction of what is socially desirable or what the examinee believes the tester likes to hear. Faking one's answers in order to create a favorable impression can be minimized in self-report inventories by means of forced-choice techniques in which the examinee is forced to select between alternatives that have been equated for social desirability. Faking is rarely a problem with mental ability tests where one knows the answer or guesses at it.

A related problem has to do with the more variable nature of what personality and motivational tests are trying to measure. The concept of "situational specificity" is used to describe the tendency for behavior to be dependent upon the context in which the person finds himself. Situational specificity is illustrated by the person who is an extrovert in the company of his peers but becomes very reserved when a superior is around.

What is the validity picture for personality or motivational tests vis-à-vis for mental ability tests? In general, the validities are seldom higher than those obtained for the more efficient, less administratively burdensome, garden variety tests of mental ability.

Nothing in this discussion implies that response tendencies represent willful and malicious acts of deception on the part of examinees. For some, response tendencies may represent momentary mechanisms for coping with unfamiliar questions; for others, they may underlie more enduring and pervasive personality characteristics with some criterion-related significance. The person, for example, who tends to endorse socially desirable items in a questionnaire may be censoring his responses in order to satisfy a broader need for conformity or social approval. There may be certain organizational contexts where the reward system favors the acquiescent worker. The issue here is not whether personality or motivational tests can be used to identify the acquiescent. This discussion suggests that response tendencies represent artifacts of measurement that make it difficult to discern enduring personality characteristics from transitory reactions to specific items.

To summarize, the tendency to fake responses in the interest of painting a favorable picture of one's self and the dynamics underlying situational specificity of responses are illustrative of the types of psychometric problems that beset the assessment of personality and motivational characteristics. To a certain extent, they can be minimized (for example, by means of forced-choice techniques) or the scores can be adjusted by means of specially devised control keys. These accommodations represent incremental costs of testing over and beyond those required by mental ability tests. The answer to the question of whether the incremental testing costs are offset by increased validity of personality or motivational measures is negative: Validities for personality tests are no higher and are frequently less than the validities obtained for paper-and-pencil ability tests. These psychometric considerations, coupled with the administrative considerations discussed earlier, account for the greater incidence of mental ability tests in the workplace.

The foregoing discussion is not intended to minimize the importance of personality and motivational variables in the workplace but only to point out both measurement and practical problems associated with their assessment and use. An ideal selection program would measure both cognitive (can do) and motivational (will do) determinants of job behavior since the use of mental ability and motivational tests in combination would enhance the accuracy with which one can predict an applicant's probable job performance. Where one must choose between mental ability or motivational tests, administrative and psychometric considerations indicate greater payoffs for using the former. The payoff associated with using paper-and-pencil, group-administered ability tests increases as the selection ratio gets smaller (indicating that there are considerably more applicants than job openings) and the tests are used to manage the flow of applicants to the more expensive modules of the employment process. This testing scenario most typically describes the employment office that handles the processing of large volumes of applicants of entry-level/high-turnover jobs.

It is recognized that there may be specific selection situations when assessment of personality and motivational characteristics is well worth the additional expense. Selection for managerial or highly technical positions is a case in point. Applicants for these positions are typically a highly select group in terms of ability dimensions (the winnowing process of graduate school, for example, will have disposed of the less able)—making ability tests inappropriate selection devices for reasons that have to do with restriction of range (see Q–46). Ability tests do not do a particularly good job of differentiating among the very able and one must consider measures showing greater variability among the applicant population of interest.

Q-10 How much subjectivity exists in the employment process?

Subjectivity can be introduced at 2 junctures of the employment process: in those modules of the employment process that are unstructured, such as the interview; and in the manner in which pre-employment information on a job candidate is combined to arrive at an overall accept or reject decision.

With respect to the first, each module in the employment process may be regarded as a way of obtaining information about the job candidate. The answer to Q–6 lists the different data acquisition mechanisms available to an employer for developing information about a prospective employee. Some of the modules are more subjective than others and, in Q–8, the discussion focused on studies that have done on the interview—a subjective selection devise used extensively to process applicants for employment. It is recalled here the general finding that introducing structure to the interviewing process enhances the reliability, validity, and usefulness of the job interview.

The second juncture of the employment process at which subjectivity can be injected has to do with the way in which information is combined into a final hiring decision. There are generally 2 ways of combining the data: They can be combined intuitively (clinical prediction) or the data can be combined according to some fixed strategy (statistical prediction) in which test scores and other pre-employment data are given pre-determined weights. It was originally hypothesized that the clinical approach that captures the nuances of the applicant's strengths and weaknesses would result in more accurate predictions (of how the applicant would subsequently behave on the job) than the more mechanistic strategy embodied in arriving at statistical predictions. The clinical prediction is, after all, an individualized prediction that is tailored to the individual's unique blend of strengths and weaknesses. Reviews comparing the 2 modes of combining data show that the more accurate results are obtained with statistical predictions in which the data are combined "by the number" (Meehl, 1954).

The discussion has distinguished between subjectivity in the data acquisition process and subjectivity in the data combination process of the employment process. In both cases, cutting down on the subjectivity by introducing greater structure to each process improves the outcome.

Q-11   What is a test battery?

Several tests may be assembled into a test battery. A person's battery score reflects his performance on all the tests used in combination. A battery score is more reliable than 1 of the component tests for reasons that have to do with utilizing more information about the person tested.

Q-12   How many tests make up the optimal test battery?

A distinction is made between an experimental test battery and an operational test battery. In a validation study, the tests administered to study subjects represent the experimental test battery. At this point in the validation process, it is not known which of the tests will work, hence the term "experimental." The purpose of the validation study is to determine which tests are sufficiently job related to merit using operationally in making employment decisions.

It is customary to include more tests in the experimental battery than one would expect to adopt in practice. The purpose is to err on the side of the overkill in order to increase the odds of coming up with a valid set of tests at the end of the criterion-related study. Tests making up the initial experimental battery are selected on the basis of the job analysis—that phase in a validation study that is concerned with determining the sets of abilities, skills, and knowledges required to perform the job in question competently. If the job analysis shows that performing numerical calculations is a significant part of what job incumbents do, a test of quantitative ability is a good bet for differentiating between the more competent workers and their less satisfactory counterparts. Whether the test in fact discerns differences in job performance is what the validation study aims to determine.

The operational test battery represents the set of tests that will be used to make employment decisions. Both statistical and practical considerations figure into the make-up and length of the operational test battery.

A validation study yields 2 sets of statistical information: zero-order validity (the extent to which each test is related to the criterion of job performance) and an intercorrelation matrix (which shows the extent to which each test is correlated with every other test). If 2 tests are highly correlated, they are measuring things in common and the inclusion of both in a battery represents needless redundancy. The ideal candidates for an operational test battery are tests with significant zero-order validities (no point in including a test that is not job related) and tests with low relationships with other tests (no point in using 2 tests that measure the same thing). The statistical rationale for combining different tests is captured by the notion that 2 heads are better than 1 (assuming that each head is not empty) if the 2 heads are different (otherwise, 1 ends up with a redundant echo). It might be indicated that elaborate statistical procedures (for example, multiple regression analysis) exist for determining the optimal length of a test battery based on statistical considerations of validity and test intercorrelations. The optimal length is reached when the point of diminishing returns is encountered: Adding more tests to a battery does not appreciably increase the prediction when the tests to be added contribute little that is unique and nonredundant.

Practical considerations also play a part in determining the length of an operational test battery. These practical considerations center on the costs of test administration for batteries of varying lengths. Each test that is added yields additional information about the examinee but it also adds to the cost of operating the employment office. It may develop that beyond a certain number of tests, the gains in prediction associated with additional tests are not justified by the additional costs of testing.

To recap, the experimental battery is composed of tests that seem logically related to the job under study. The make-up of this provisional battery is determined by the outcome of the job analysis phase of test validation where employee characteristics for successful job performance are identified. A validation study is conducted to generate the empirical data for determining which tests in the experimental battery are going to be useful predictors of job performance. Statistical and practical considerations are taken into account in assembling the set of tests that will comprise the operational test battery recommended for everyday use.

Q-13 What strategies exist for combining information from different tests?

Two general strategies or decision rules exist for acting on the results of several tests. In the multiple cutoff approach, threshold requirements on each test are set and the job candidate must meet or exceed the minimum qualifying score on each of the tests in order to proceed to the next step in the employment process. Put another way, any candidate who "fails" any of the tests is not considered further. In the multiple regression strategy, the standards are based on the entire battery rather than on a single component test. The multiple regression strategy is said to be compensatory

The 1970 version of the EEOC guidelines on testing contains a passage that comes close to expressing our sentiments:

§1607.1 Statement of Purpose

(a) The Guidelines in this part are based on the belief that properly validated and standardized employee selection procedures can significantly contribute to the implementation of nondiscriminatory personnel policies, as required by Title VII. It is also recognized that professionally developed tests, when used in conjunction with other tools of personnel assessment and complemented by sound programs of job design, may significantly aid in the development and maintenance of an efficient work force and, indeed, aid in the utilization and conservation of human resources generally.

No intrinsic contradition is seen between the use of professionally developed and validated selection procedures and the attainment of affirmative action objectives. It may be instructive to look at the experience of the American Telephone and Telegraph Company, which signed a consent decree with the federal government (EEOC and the Departments of Justice and Labor). The consent decree stipulated in part that:

Each Bell Company may continue to utilize test scores on validated tests along with other job-related considerations in assessing individual qualifications. However, no Bell Company shall rely upon the minimum scores required or preferred on its pre-employment aptitude test batteries as justification for its failure to meet its intermediate targets for any job classification. (Section 5, page 9)

Throughout the 6-year life of the consent decree, units of the Bell System continued the use of validated tests for selection and promotion purposes and carried out other consent decree provisions aimed at increasing the utilization of minorities and women. In their report to the U.S. District Court in Philadelphia, attorneys for the government stated that AT&T and its associated Bell operating companies were in substantial compliance, meeting more than 98% of their hiring and promotion targets or numerical objectives (Daily Labor Report, no. 13, January 18, 1979).

There is at least 1 major corporation whose affirmative action obligations have been met without giving up its testing program.

How did AT&T do it? Charles Brown, AT&T's chairman of the board in an address before the National Urban League conference in 1980 described the process in the following way:

Businesslike. That's still a term—despite the disfavor in which the public is said to hold business these days—that has positive connotations. It means actions that produce results without a lot of fuss and without much concern as to who gets credit for it.

I am not going to pretend to you that the notion of goals and timetables wasn't an uncomfortable one for us when it first emerged. Once, however, we were persuaded that progress in equal opportunity—like progress in most everything else—depended on knowing what objectives we wanted to reach by when, we set about—as good business practice requires—developing the methods and procedures, the management instructions, the measurement plans and the tracking procedures—in short, the routines to assure that the job got done.

By fostering businesslike programs like those I have in mind, programs based on candid cost-benefit analysis and equipped with tracking mechanisms that promptly distinguish what works from what doesn't—we may be able to accomplish in the '80s what in the '70s we failed to accomplish. Looking backward, it seems to me that the '70s represent not so much a failure of national will as a failure of management. We can—we must—manage better.

Q-17 How does an organization decide whether it needs a testing program?

An organization contemplating installing a testing program for selection purposes needs to answer 2 questions in the affirmative: Do I need it? Can I support the effort?

With respect to the first question, the need for a testing program increases as the volume of employment activity increases and as the need to upgrade the quality of the human intake increases. In the situation where a quantitative increase in processing of job candidates is anticipated, the testing program provides an efficient mechanism for managing applicant flow. The second situation involves a qualitative increase in the caliber of the human input and may arise due to the inadequacy or erosion of existing selection procedures or to changes in job requirements brought about by the introduction of advanced machine systems. Thus, qualitative or quantitative factors may create the felt need for installing a testing program.

The second question has to do with having the necessary support mechanisms in place for mounting the validation effort, implementing the validated products in the workplace, and maintaining the integrity of the testing enterprise in everyday usage. There is more to maintaining the viability of a testing program than a stopwatch, a few test booklets, and a supply of answer sheets!

Two observations: The days for installing employment tests in order to "keep up with the Joneses" are probably behind us. In today's environment, organizations that use tests out of sense that it is the fashionable thing to do incur legal exposure sufficient to discourage the effort. The potential damage to the employment opportunities of minority applicants inflicted by unvalidated tests should touch the moral conscience of the most fashion conscious. When the foregoing considerations operate to restrict the use of tests to those situations that are justified by business necessity, employment testing will have found its rightful place.

The second observation says that the payoffs associated with a testing program tend to be long term and diffuse. For example, the effects associated with a testing program that is set up to screen for higher skills required by advanced machine systems are likely to be melded into the benefits attributed to technology. Under these conditions, machine effects and testing effects are said to be confounded. Even if the beneficial effects due to testing could be isolated and quantified, it is not likely that the benefits will be registered overnight. The point of this tale is not to extol the virtues of patience and perseverance but to caution against unrealistic expectations with respect to the gains associated with testing and how soon these gains may be realized. Testing is not geared to provide quick fixes.

Q-18 How much technical training does a testing program require?

The 2 generic aspects of a sound testing program involve test research and development and test administration. The test research aspect is concerned with the technical quality of the tests that are used and with the adequacy of the validation study to support the test's use. Competent performance of these technical activities requires formal training, usually up to the Ph.D. level. The requirement for a high level of expertise in the selection research area is highlighted by the possibility of litigation and the attendant need for an expert witness with credible credentials. It might be pointed out that various portions of the test research requirements may be contracted out. Reputable test publishers exist that can provide a wide selection of tests with the requisite test development information. The availability of these tests "off the shelf" relieves the user of the need to develop his homegrown devices. Similarly, there are consulting firms whose services include the conduct of validation studies. Behavioral scientists in the academic world are another source of external expertise. Even when the technical aspects of a testing program are farmed out, however, it helps to have in-house expertise to assist in the selection of suitable consultants and to act as study monitor.

Test administration encompasses the support activities required to implement the tests in the work setting. When the tests are in the process of being validated, the test administration function involves administering the experimental test battery to study subjects. After the validation study is completed, the test administration function may range from such mundane tasks as keeping an adequate supply of test booklets and answer sheets in stock to developing policies and procedures for retesting of unsuccessful examinees or treatment of borderline testing cases. In multiunit organizations, test administration may involve determining whether the test is appropriate for jobs that have the same titles across locations but that are configured differently to accommodate local requirements. Day-to-day questions of test implementation take in the full range of decisions. They are best addressed when the test administrator works in tandem with the professional who developed and validated the test.

Q-19 Wouldn't a dangerous precedent be set if employment managers waived test qualification standards?

This book does not advocate that established test standards be waived for frivolous reasons. It is urged that decision makers be open to the possibility that under certain circumstances, nontest credentials may be sufficiently strong to compensate for an otherwise failing score on a pre-employment test. When the reasons for waiving test standards are reasonable and the transaction is properly documented, the precedent that is set is one in which test information is intelligently weighed vis-à-vis other indicators of job success. This practice is hardly dangerous; it is very practical and downright sensible.

Q-20 Should all applicants be evaluated using the "whole person" approach?

Ideally, all applicants should be looked at from a whole person point of view and the accept/reject decision should be made on the basis of the applicant's overall qualifications. This practice is consistent with the general proposition that the more information is known about a person, the better the resulting decision.

In the real world, there are 2 major constraints that do not make it practical to assess the overall qualifications of applicants for employment. One constraint has to do with the volume of employment activity: When large numbers of applicants need to be processed or when the entire employment process incorporates an expensive module (for example, assessment techniques or work simulations), it may be necessary to install a front-end mechanism for managing applicant flow. The other constraint has to do with situations in which deficiencies in certain skills or abilities cannot be compensated for by strengths in other skills or abilities. A wholesome personality, for example, is not likely to make up for poor driving skills among applicants for interstate truck driver positions (see discussion of multiple cutoff, *Q-13*).

Both constraints make it practically infeasible to subject all job candidates to the end-to-end processing that yields all the data needed to evaluate their overall qualifications. Under these circumstances, a sequential screening strategy is typically adopted in which applicants who fail one module in the employment process are disqualified from further consideration.

What to do with borderline cases—those who are just below the established qualification level? Even when a sequential screen is indicated, borderline cases should be given a closer look. The closer look might indicate that retesting is warranted or it may lead to the conclusion that rejection is in order. In either case, a closer examination of the borderline cases is a reasonable recognition that job qualifications are occasionally packaged in a way that eludes decision-making rules that have been set up "by the number."

Q-21 *How are passing scores set?*

There are 2 separate processes that are involved in a validation study. One has to do with determining whether a test is job related (Do policemen need to understand English?); the other deals with establishing cutoff scores or test qualification standards for operational use (Do policemen need to understand Shakespeare?). The discussion is concerned with the latter.

The general strategy for setting cutoff scores is a judgmental process that takes a number of nontest factors into account. The process of setting cutoff scores is less straightforward than the process of showing job relatedness. In the discussion of practical utility (see *Q-60*), the notion is introduced of an institutional expectancy chart to call attention to 2 major consequences of setting a cutoff score. Reference to Figure 2 will show that any given cutoff score yields a payoff on the criterion of job performance (the proportion of selectees who are satisfactory workers on the job) and a selection ratio (the proportion of examinees who are able to meet the test qualification standard). Balancing criterion payoffs with realistic selection ratios figures prominently in the decision to set cutoff scores. It is a decision that is best made jointly by the client or departmental representative who speaks to the calibre of job performance that the testing program should be geared to achieving and by the personnel or human resources manager who speaks to the employment, recruitment, and EEO implications of setting cutoff scores of varying severity. Both inputs are relevant.

The discussion is intended to show that there is no absolute demarcation line on the test score distribution that sorts out all the good job performers from their unsuccessful counterparts, just as there is no magical break on the height dimension in reference to which one is considered either tall or short. In both situations, however, there is a zone of reasonableness that is associated with test qualified persons or with tall persons. Narrowing the zone down to an operational cutoff score that is appropriate to the test user's particular circumstances is a judgment call. This judgment is most competently and responsibly made when information is known about criterion payoffs, selection ratios, cost of testing, adequacy of training programs to remedy initially erroneous hiring decisions, and the employer's affirmative action commitments.

It should be noted that the decision to hire someone who has met all the pre-employment selection hurdles does not end the selection process. The new hire continues to be evaluated as he learns the organizational ropes and the terms of the employer-employee contract are played out in various training and on-the-job scenarios. The probationary period for a new employee continues well into the job. Newly hired employees could find themselves without a job if they fail to successfully complete the company's training program or if they violate policies and practices governing acceptable work behavior. In short, on-the-job measures exist for remedying erroneous hiring decisions.

It also should be noted that whenever a cutoff score is set, some will manage to barely pass and some will manage to barely fail it. Sliding the cutoff score higher or lower will not solve the problem; it will merely change the identities of the near passes and the near failures. In school settings, the difference between a low A and a high B can become thin and bothersome. For these borderline cases, obtaining additional nontest information to supplement test data in arriving at the overall qualification picture is a sensible practice (see *Q–20*).

To summarize, there is no magical point in the test score distribution that defines the cutoff score. Establishing a test qualification standard that is suitable for operational use in the context of a company's particular set of circumstances requires the exercise of good judgment. Considerations involving selection ratios, criterion payoffs, costs of recruiting and testing, affirmative action commitments, efficacy of on-the-job measures to counteract erroneous placements are relevant input to the decision about where to locate the cutoff score.

Q–22 Is the process of establishing cutoff scores an arbitrary process?

There is a world of difference between good faith efforts to use judgment in doing the best with what one has and the aimless indifference that is associated with caprice. This distinction is best captured by W. Popham (1978):

Unable to avoid reliance on human judgment as the chief ingredient in standard-setting, some individuals have thrown up their hands in dismay and cast aside all efforts to set performance standards as *arbitrary,* hence unacceptable.

But *Webster's Dictionary* offers us two definitions of arbitrary. The first of these is positive, describing arbitrary as an adjective reflecting choice or discretion, that is "determinable by a judge or tribunal." The second definition, pejorative in nature, describes arbitrary as an adjective denoting capriciousness, that is, "selected at random and without reason." In my estimate, when people start knocking the standard-setting game as arbitrary, they are clearly employing Webster's second, negatively loaded definition.

But the first definition is more accurately reflective of serious standard-setting effort. They represent genuine attempts to do a good job in deciding what kinds of standards we ought to employ. That they are judgmental is inescapable. But to malign all judgmental operations as capricious is absurd. (p. 168)

Q-23 Should test scores be used on a rank order or on a pass/fail basis?

One way to avoid setting a cutoff score on the test is to make selections based on a rank ordering of how applicants performed on the test. If, for example, there are 5 vacancies to be filled, job candidates could be ranked from highest to lowest test scorers and the top 5 test scorers would be considered.

An alternative strategy would set qualification bands based on ranges of test scores, with no further distinction made among examinees falling within a particular qualification category. The table below illustrates the concept of using successive cuts on the test score distribution to define 3 qualification levels:

Qualification Status	Score Ranges
Test qualified	20 and above
Intermediate	15 – 19
Not test qualified	14 and below

In the example, the person who scores 20 on the test is considered just as test qualified as the person with a test score of 25 or 30—both are placed in the test qualified pool. The probability of being selected, given that one is in the test qualified pool by virtue of having scored 20 or higher on the test, would depend on factors such as relevance of work experience, specific training, pre-employment interview results, and other nontest employment criteria.

Rank ordering or the use of qualification zones represent 2 distinct strategies for utilizing test performance data in filling personnel requisitions. There are certain points of similarities and differences between the two approaches. Both assume that the relationship between test performance and performance on the job is linear such that the higher the test performance, the better the job performance. The notion of linearity is not difficult to see with content valid tests, such as typing test. The examinee who scores 45 words per minute (WPM) on the test will tend to be more proficient on the job than an examinee who types 43 WPM who, in turn, is more proficient than one who scores 40 WPM.

The use of rank-ordering strategies results in a dynamic list of job candidates ready for placement: The person who is at the top of the list today could be displaced from that position tomorrow by an even higher scoring examinee. On the other hand, when broad qualification zones are used, the person who is test qualified retains that status for as long as the test standards are in force. His chances of placement relative to some other candidate scoring numerically higher in the same qualification zone depends on factors other than differences in their raw or numerical test scores. This mundane difference may have implications for computing qualification rates on the test or for complying with contractual agreement with unions that has to do with the use of the test as an absolute disqualifier. It should be noted that the person who scores very poorly on the test is not likely to be helped by either strategy under normal labor market conditions.

When there are differences in test performance between 2 groups, the use of ranking will tend to exaggerate the differences and lead to reduced selection rate for members of the lower scoring group. The use of broad qualification categories, on the other hand, disregards numerical differences among those falling within the same zone, thereby attenuating some of the differences between the 2 groups.

A concluding comment: Rank ordering of job candidates on the basis of their test scores places much greater weight on the test than the use of broad test qualification categories. Assuming linearity of relationship between test performance and job performance, it is true that the person who scores 45 WPM will, on the average and over many selection decisions, be more proficient than the person who scores 40 or 44 WPM. Whether the difference in payoff is sufficient to warrant the use of rank-ordering strategies in light of the average level of test validity (see *Q–63*), in light of known group differences in test performance between minorities and nonminorities (see *Q–66*) and in light of the sensible use of nontest information to determine overall job suitability (see *Q–20*), is in the nature of an administrative decision that goes beyond statistical considerations of linearity. In most circumstances, the use of broad qualification zones is both responsible and prudent—a practice that allows employers to reap the benefits of a validated testing program and to discharge its responsibilities as corporate citizens.

Q–24 Should tests be geared toward measuring entry-level qualifications or beyond?

The general proposition is that tests should be geared to meeting reasonable and realistic staffing objectives. Extreme situations are easy to spot: the first-day-on-the-job syndrome in which tests are used to predict performance during the period of orientation or initiation into the company and the chairman-of-the-board syndrome in which applicants for entry-level job are evaluated for qualifications normally associated with officer positions.

Guidance on what is realistic is discernible from the *Uniform Guidelines:*

Sec. 5. (I). Use of selection procedures for higher level jobs. If job progression structures are so established that employees will probably, within a reasonable period of time and in a majority of cases, progress to a higher level, it may be considered that the applicants are being evaluated for a job or jobs at the higher level. However, where job progression is not so nearly automatic, or the time span is such that the higher level jobs or employees' potential may be expected to change in significant ways, it should be considered that applicants are being evaluated for a job at or near the entry level. A "reasonable period of time" will vary for different jobs and employment situations but will seldom be more than 5 years. Use of selection procedures to evaluate applicants for a higher level job would not be appropriate:

(1) If the majority of those remaining employed do not progress to the higher level job;
(2) If there is reason to doubt that the higher level job will continue to require essentially similar skills during the progression period; or
(3) If the selection procedures measure knowledges, skills, or abilities required for advancement which would be expected to develop principally from the training or experience on the job.

Q-25 What do the Uniform Guidelines have to say about passing scores?

The most relevant provisions occur in the following provisions of the *Uniform Guidelines:*

Sec. 5. (G). *Method of use of selection procedures.* The evidence of both the validity and utility of a selection procedure should support the method the user chooses for operational use of the procedure, if that method of use has a greater adverse impact than another method of use. Evidence which may be sufficient to support the use of a selection procedure on a pass/fail (screening) basis may be insufficient to support a ranking basis under these guidelines. Thus, if a user decides to use a selection procedure on a ranking basis, and that method of use has a greater adverse impact than use on an appropriate pass/fail basis (see section 5H below), the user should have sufficient evidence of validity and utility to support the use on a ranking basis. See sections 3B, 14B (5) and (6), and 14C (8) and (9).

Sec. 5. (H). *Cutoff scores.* Where cutoff scores are used, they should normally be set as to be reasonable and consistent with normal expectations of acceptable proficiency within the work force. Where applicants are ranked on the basis of properly validated selection procedures and those applicants scoring below a higher cutoff score than appropriate in light of such expectations have little or no chance of being selected for employment, the higher cutoff score may be appropriate, but the degree of adverse impact should be considered.

Q-26 What is a manager to do with tests that are valid for whites but not for blacks or vice versa?

Empirical studies investigating the question of whether tests work the same way for various groups have generally found that tests that are valid for whites also tend to be valid for blacks (see *Q-66*). This finding, based on enough studies to render it professionally respectable, is welcomed on several fronts. On logical grounds, one would expect—and the studies confirm—that a job that requires a particular attribute for competent performance would require it of all incumbents, regardless of their race, sex, national origin, or religious affiliation. Theoretically, it makes for coherence and parsimony to explain the same behavior (job performance) with the same set of constructs (characteristics measured by the tests). Procedurally, the day-to-day operations of an employment office is helped if the same tests were administered to all applicants vying for the same job.

With the foregoing as background, the situation posed in the question is anomalous but not impossible. That is to say, the question addresses the exception rather than the rule. As a first step, the manager should rule out the possibility that the depressed validities obtained for 1 group but not for others are not attributable to statistical artifacts such as restriction of range or unreliability of measurement that are unique to the 1 group for which the test shows no validity (see *Q-58*). If this sleuth work yields no statistical culprits, the manager may have to bite the bullet by using the test only for the group for which it is valid, leaving other selection procedures (for example, the interview) work harder for the untested group(s). If the volume of employment activity warrants it, the long-term solution might be to undertake another validation study with a view toward coming up with a common battery of tests appropriate for all applicant groups.

Q-27 Where does the heredity versus environment debate leave today's managers?

Elsewhere the view was expressed that managers can competently and responsibly carry out their duties in the human resources area without knowing the precise blend of genetic and environmental factors for observed group differences in test performance (see *Q-71*). In the real world, the manager with an employment office to run is faced with the prospect of doing the best he can with what he's got. He has no control over the genetic make-up of the applicants that show up at his employment office and he has little control over their experiential backgrounds. He has no say over the chromosomal endowment of his potential employees or the lifelong history of reinforcement that shaped their present behavior. But the manager does have control over organizational resources that can be applied to decisions that range from those that determine who gets employed and who does not to those that govern which skills ought to be enhanced via training and which employees would profit most from structured developmental programs. In short, while the manager may not be able to control the genetic or environmental origins that underlie individual differences, he can recognize them in committing corporate resources and support systems to those discretionary choices that have to do with enlarging the collective and individual competencies of the organization's human resources. Stated differently, even if the basis of group differences in test performance were known with precision, it is likely that the manager in the real world will find the information of limited academic value.

Q-28   What do the Uniform Guidelines on Employee Selection Procedures have to say about the heredity versus environment debate as it relates to employment tests?

The *Uniform Guidelines* are silent on this issue.

Q-29   What are the consequences of using an invalid test?

An invalid test is one that is not predictive of or related to job performance. This means that high test scorers are no more likely to do well on the job than low scorers. The major consequences of using an invalid test are 2:

A.   From a business point of view, use of the invalid test to make selection decisions would not meet the employer's legitimate interest in hiring people who can do the job. To the applicant who goes through the ritual of being tested, the invalid test represents an irrelevant step in the employment process.

B.   From a legal point of view, use of an invalid test exposes the employer to employment discrimination lawsuits. In these lawsuits, defendant's burden of showing the job relatedness of challenged employment tests is a heavy one even when a competently conducted validation study supports test use; without a validation study, the legal issue is transformed into one of damages and awards.

Q-30   Does test performance decline with age?

The first answers to this question were a resounding "yes" based on data that showed that the average test scores of older examinees were lower than the average test scores of younger groups of examinees. These data were obtained from cross-sectional studies in which groups of examinees at different age levels were tested at the same point in time. Cross-sectional studies represented the early inquiries into the relationship between test performance and age and the outcome was decidedly in the direction of declining test performance with increase in age.

Longitudinal studies represent another way of studying the same problem. In longitudinal designs, the same study subjects are tracked and tested over their life courses. Instead of comparing 50-year-olds with a younger generation of 30-year-olds as in cross-sectional studies, the comparisons in longitudinal designs involve the test performance of the

50-year-olds today with the same persons tested 20 years ago. Longitudinal studies show that some abilities (for example, verbal) improve with age, while others (for example, perceptual or motor skills) decline with age, although the decrement is not nearly as pronounced as what cross-sectional studies show.

A better picture is obtained when the 2 types of studies are combined in a joint cross-sectional and longitudinal design, such as that performed by K. Schaie and G. Lavouvie-Vief (1974). The results of their study show the predictable differences between age-groups that are observed in cross-sectional studies and the fairly constant performance within each age group that is observed in longitudinal designs. In other words, many older subjects performed at least as well as they did when they were younger, but the young generation today performs better than their counterparts of 30 years ago.

A few items to keep in mind when evaluating studies dealing with the effects of age on test performance: First, people who differ in age frequently differ in other characteristics, such as level of educational attainment or access to information provided by TV and other mass media. The sorts of differences between generations that are picked up in cross-sectional studies represent differences in life experiences. Instead of age differences in test performance, it may be more meaningful to speak of generational differences in test performance to call attention to test-affecting events that occur through time rather than the mere ticking of the clock. Second, the differential decline in abilities (that is, some abilities decline while others do not) suggests that practiced abilities are maintained better and longer than abilities that suffer from disuse. The cumulative experiences of adulthood enhance the development of certain abilities and skills relative to others. Hence, the question of whether test performance deteriorates with age is best answered when the kinds of abilities tested are specified. Third, researchers are impressed by the range of individual differences in the groups studied. To quote Schaie:

All of the material presented above, of course, refers to findings on groups of people. What about the range of individual differences? While it does not follow that all old people have declined intellectually, some indeed have, but so have some people at age 30. Our longitudinal studies of individuals show that we have some remarkable individuals who gained in level of performance from age 70 to age 84; others have declined from age 20 to age 30. (p. 121)

To summarize, the extent to which test performance declines with age depends on whether cross-sectional or longitudinal comparisons are made. In general, cross-sectional studies show more pronounced age group differences than longitudinal studies. The trend of declining test performance with advancing age is better understood within a framework that takes into account the differences between generations in life experiences, the role of practice in the differential maintenance of certain abilities, and the wide range of variation in the groups studied.

In closing, it is noted that most of the discussion is based on studies that have dealt with ability or cognitive tests. The competent adult is viewed as one who has developed a strategy for effectively coping with his environment's intellective, affective, and interpersonal demands. Ability factors of the sort used in research studies concerned with the effects of aging are seen as occupying some, but not the entire, space in the spectrum of the adult's repertoire. Experiential strategies, crystallized through the years of training and on-the-job behavior, represent the other elements in the spectrum.

Q-31 Should adjustment in test scores be made for older examinees?

The suggestion has been made that the test scores of older examinees be adjusted upward to compensate for age-related decrement in test performance. The suggestion recognizes that in most employment situations, the older job candidate is competing against younger applicants who enjoy the advantages of belonging to the younger generation. That is to say, cross-sectional rather than longitudinal comparisons are relevant in the employment setting and the outcome of cross-sectional studies almost uniformly shows generational differences in favor of younger examinees.

Adjusting test scores because of generational differences in test performance fails to take into account possible generational differences in job performance. A variable such as age or ethnic group membership, which operates to lower the test scores of older or minority examinees, may operate in the same way to lower their job performance, thereby contributing to the valid variance. If the group that scores low on a valid test obtains a correspondingly low score on the criterion measure of job performance, no adjustment in test score differential between the 2 groups is necessary (see *Q-71* on differential validity and *Q-68*, which discusses how differences in test scores do not necessarily mean that the test is biased).

An alternative approach would look at the older person's test performance in conjunction with other evidences of his ability to do the job. This whole person view may reveal established funds of knowledge and resources in the older person's work history that may compensate for his test score (see *Q-20*).

Q-32 Does the Age Discrimination in Employment Act prohibit the use of tests for older job candidates?

Enacted in 1967 and amended in 1978, the Age Discrimination in Employment Act (ADEA) prohibits employment discrimination against persons who are between the ages of 40 to 70. The thrust of ADEA was to require that employment decisions involving persons in the protected age bracket be based on their ability to do the job rather on their age. The Department of Labor was initially empowered to administer and enforce ADEA until July 1979 when the functions were transferred to EEOC.

The issue of employment testing under ADEA has been addressed by each of the 2 agencies entrusted with administering the Act. In 1968, the Age and Hour Division of the Department of Labor published some interpretive guidelines that include a section on testing:

Sec. 860.104 (b) *Employee testing.* The use of a validated employee test is not, of itself, a violation of the Act when such test is specifically related to the requirements of the job, is fair and reasonable, is administered in good faith and without discrimination on the basis of age, and is properly evaluated. A vital factor in employee testing as it relates to the 40-65 age group protected by the statute is the "test sophistication" or "test wiseness" of the individual. Younger persons, due to the tremendous increase in the use of tests in primary and secondary schools in recent years, may generally have had more experience in test-taking than older individuals and, consequently, where an employee test is used as the sole tool or the controlling factor in the employee selection procedure, such younger persons may have an advantage over older applicants who may have had considerable on-the-job experience but who, due to age, are further removed from their schooling. Therefore, situations in which an employee test is used as the sole tool or the controlling factor in the employee selection procedure will be carefully scrutinized to ensure that the test is for a permissible purpose and not for purposes prohibited by the statute.

The EEOC, which inherited administration of the ADEA from the Department of Labor, addressed the testing issue in the following language from the *Uniform Guidelines on Employee Selection Procedures:*

Sec. 2 (D) Limitations. These guidelines apply only to persons subject to Title VII, Executive Order 11246, or other equal employment opportunity requirements of Federal law. These guidelines do not apply to responsibilities under the Age Discrimination in Employment Act of 1967, as amended, not to discriminate on the basis of age, or under sections 501, 503, and 504 of the Rehabilitation Act of 1973, not to discriminate on the basis of handicap.

The foregoing passages provide limited guidance to the practitioner. Developments in the legal realm are no more helpful for, although Title VII sent 3 "testing" cases to the Supreme Court (*Griggs v. Duke Power, Albemarle Paper Co. v. Moody,* and *Washington v. Davis*), testing under ADEA is substantially unlitigated. It is strongly recommended that tests used for making employment decisions be validated. It is believed that a competent validation study coupled with prudent test administration practices will go a long way toward satisfying the interpretive guidelines enunciated by the Department of Labor, "such test is specifically related to the requirements of the job, is fair and reasonable, is administered in good faith and without discrimination on the basis of age, and is properly evaluated."

Q-33   Does employment testing breed conformity?

The notion that psychological tests could be used to generate conformity is 1 commonly held misconception of psychological measurement. In the employment context, the criticism is directed at the use of pre-employment tests to select applicants with certain specified characteristics that are compatible with the "party line." Traits such as dominance, submissiveness, sales savvy, and flexibility seem to be among the most highly valued.

The response has 3 elements. To begin, it is observed that the tendency to cultivate conformity in the sense of selectively reinforcing certain normative behaviors is not unique to the employment setting. The definition of what is and what is not acceptable behavior characterizes all human interaction. It is, therefore, not surprising to find conformity in prison cells as well as in monasteries. The more substantive question is not whether conformity exists but conformity to what? If the conformity is to a set of behaviors that are conducive to culturally defined success, perhaps this is the kind of conformity that achievement-oriented societies ought to nurture and encourage.

Second, it is noted that pre-employment tests typically deal with the more cognitive job requirements rather than the personality or motivational characteristics of job applicants for reasons elaborated upon in Q-9. The use of ability tests as selection devices will generate the same conformity to improved job performance as personality tests, yet the charges of conformity are associated only with the latter. (It is assumed that both types of tests have been validated against the same criterion of job performance.) There seems to be a feeling that the technology of measuring personality characteristics has reached a level of sophistication that makes possible the systematic selection of the conforming job applicant. It is noted elsewhere (see Q-9) that personality assessment is beset with a number of measurement problems, making their use as selection devices inadvisable except in special situations. Even where a validated and operational test battery includes personality or motivational tests, "passing" scores can be obtained in a number of ways and through a multitude of response patterns so that about the only common characteristic of high test scorers is that they have a higher probability of job success than their lower test scoring counterparts.

Last, the author is not unaware of impressions and anecdotes to the effect that certain types of individuals seem to be identified with certain organizations. The "organization man" seems to assimilate the dominant characteristics imputed to the organization that employs him. It is believed that his phenomenon, to the extent that it exists, has to do more with the reward structure of the employing organization than with its pre-employment criteria. In other words, felt pressures in the workplace shape and mold behavior more than the selection devices in the employment office.

Q-34 The preceding question suggests that tests are not held in high regard by the public. Why is this so?

For at least the following reasons:

(1) Tests have been abused before, the abuses have been highlighted in popular books, and readers remember. It is recalled here the observation made earlier: A doctor is sued for malpractice not for the 999 successful operations but for the 1 instance of professional inadvertence.

(2) The technology associated with test development and test usage is technical and complex. Test specialists have not been particularly assiduous or successful in their efforts to communicate testing matters in language that facilitate understanding.

(3) Tests are not the object of uniform admiration because they tell us unpopular things about our world and about ourselves. Test scores mirror deficiencies in our educational system, reflect misplaced priorities, register the outcome of social programs that did not work, and document the gap between bold dreams and unforgiving realities. In the employment setting, personnel managers may find themselves using tests as crutches rather than as aids to decision making, thereby abdicating their judgments in favor of the magical number represented by a test cutoff score.

The rejoinders, in the form of analogies, are by now familiar. One does not get rid of a thermometer because it shows that the patient has a fever nor does one kill the messenger that bears the bad news.

Elsewhere (see *Q-35*) the view has been expressed that extreme pre-occupation with group differences in test performance can lead to an impasse in which salvos of rejoinders and counterrejoinders are exchanged without apparent regard to broader issues of human resources utilization that a test-using employer must contend with. The view of this author does not imply any resignation over a bad state of affairs that is not destined to get any better but rather a recognition that the present state of affairs, such as they are, will be with us for some time to come.

Q-35 Should there be a moratorium on employment testing?

The moratorium should be imposed on test abuse, including practices that involve:

- The use of unvalidated tests. To paraphrase the opinion of the Supreme Court in *Griggs v. Duke Power Company* (401 U.S. 424 (1971)): Unless they were demonstrably related to job performance, employment procedures and testing mechanisms could operate as "built-in headwinds" for minority groups.

- A Freudian fixation on group differences in test performance along with the pre-occupation with the genetic or environmental determinants of observed group differences (see *Q-71*).

- Overinterpretation of test scores (see *Q-71*) in which test scores are given such controlling force that tests become crutches rather than tools for decision-making purposes (see *Q-34*).

It has been indicated that professionally validated tests can be useful in making selection decisions by providing standardized measures of job qualifications to serve as a basis for determining who gets accepted and who gets rejected among applicants vying for a limited number of openings. In a selection situation where many are called but not all can be chosen, some means must be found for deciding who gets selected. Under these circumstances, tests have several features to recommend themselves:

- Tests provide a standardized and common metric for measuring relevant job qualifications.

- Tests of the paper-and-pencil variety provide an efficient mechanism for managing applicant flow.

- Tests enjoy procedural advantages over the typical unstructured employment interview or the glittering letter of recommendation in terms of administration, scoring, and interpretation.

- Tests provide an objective yardstick less susceptible to favoritism or social stereotyping that characterizes more subjective evaluations of human behavior. It is probably true that the standardized employment test in comparison with other methods of assessing applicant characteristics is, to paraphrase J. Gardner (1961, p. 48), less likely to see whether the examinee was in rags or in tweeds and less likely to hear the accent of the slums.

Those advocating doing away with testing altogether are faced with the need to recommend more suitable alternatives. Invariably, these nontest alternatives must answer the bottom-line question of whether they are any more valid, any more administratively feasible, and any more legally defensible than the devices they seek to replace. It is suspected that these alternative selection procedures are most suitably used in conjunction with, rather than instead of, employment tests.

Q-36 Is it better to validate a test or minimize its adverse impact?

Developments surrounding equal employment laws have linked the concepts of adverse impact and validity in a relationship approximated by the following scenario: A particular selection procedure becomes suspect when it has an adverse impact on the employment opportunities of protected groups. Adverse impact may be shown by statistics that reveal that use of the selection procedure has resulted in substantial disparities in hiring rates or, where employment testing is the issue, in pass rates between minorities and nonminorities. A showing of adverse impact generally triggers the requirement for a showing that the procedure in question is job related and justified by business necessity. Where tests are involved, job relatedness is most frequently shown by means of a validation study. Thus, adverse impact of a test triggers the requirement for a showing of the test's validity. Put another way, there is no legal obligation to validate a procedure whose application does not adversely affect protected group members.

Against the foregoing background, the question assumes an either-or character: Should a test user put all the eggs in the validity basket or in the adverse impact basket? The answer has the following elements.

The view is that validity is good business in the sense that using a test that measures relevant job requirements identifies job candidates qualified to do what is good for the business. Therefore, organizations contemplating the use of tests to make selection decisions should make every effort to validate them. (It is assumed that a validation study is technically feasible. See *Q-46*.) If the outcome of the validation study shows that a particular test is not valid or is no longer valid, the next agenda item for the business minded is to find one that is valid. One additional consideration: In today's world where every personnel decision is potentially a legal transaction, having validity information for selection procedures in use also serves the additional purpose of giving the company a measure of protection in a legal proceeding. In short, what does test validity buy? It meets the human resources requirements for identifying qualified personnel to operate the business and it additionally provides the evidence of job relatedness that the employer needs in the event of an employment discrimination lawsuit.

Next discussed is the basket labelled adverse impact. The discussion is started by noting that adverse impact is not an unambiguous concept. As noted in *Q-94*, there are alternative ways of measuring adverse impact so that for the same set of data, different ways of measuring adverse impact may yield different pictures. Furthermore, the quantum problem involves the question of how much adverse impact (however this may be measured) needs to be shown in order to trigger the requirement for validation. The courts have addressed the quantum problem in fairly imprecise terms. The *Uniform Guidelines* provide some guidance by advocating the 4/5ths rule of thumb. While the 4/5ths rule is quantitative enough, it is, however, only a rule of thumb. It is not clear, for example, whether adverse impact is present in situations where the differences between the comparison groups are within the 4/5ths rule but reach levels that are statistically significant. In addition to being shrouded in ambiguity, the concept of adverse impact is also a dynamic concept. A multiunit organization using the same test for selection purposes may find that adverse impact is present in 1 location but not in another or that adverse impact is present in the same location for 1 period of time but not for another period of time. The picture gets fuzzier when it is found that adverse impact is present in 1 location but not in another when the test of statistical significance is applied to group differences in pass rates even though the disparities in fail rates are within the 4/5ths rule of thumb. Which particular location, which particular time frame, and which particular metric are relevant may be determined by circumstances beyond the test user's control—such as those surrounding a complaining party's case and precipitating an unfair discrimination lawsuit. Because of the dynamic nature of adverse impact, it is difficult for the most prudent managers to plan for it. Validity, on the other hand, is established using fairly straightforward and commonly acceptable procedures. More importantly, once the validity of a test is established, the validity information "keeps."

For the considerations discussed above, it is believed that there are strategic advantages to placing the eggs in the basket labelled validity. In the same breath, it is acknowledged that the reduction of adverse impact provides the test user with another option. The ideal situation, of course, is one where a test user has testing devices that are supported by solid validity data and complemented by what AT&T's chairman calls "business-like programs with timetables and instructions" designed to minimize the impact of tests on the company's affirmative action responsibilities. As the discussion in *Q-16* makes clear, it is not believed that testing and affirmative action are mutually exclusive. Indeed, the chances that affirmative action requirements become a part of the business become enhanced when business becomes a part of affirmative action.

Part II

EMPLOYMENT TESTING—
THE PSYCHOMETRIC CONTEXT

Q-37 *What is the meaning of test validity?*

The basic notion behind validity is the notion of job relatedness: An employment test is said to be valid if it measures the abilities, skills, and worker characteristics related to the job in question. In other words, a test is valid if persons who score low on the test tend to perform poorly on the job and persons who score high on the test tend to perform successfully on the job. It is the relationship or correlation between test performance and job performance that underlies the basic concept of validity.

Q-38 *Why is validity important?*

For 2 reasons: First, from a business point of view, validity ensures that decisions are made on the basis of job-relevant standards. Second, from a legal point of view, validity information increases the probability of successfully surviving time-consuming and potentially expensive employment discrimination lawsuits.

Q-39 *How many ways are there of validating a test?*

There are 3 major methods of validating a test for its job relatedness: construct, content, and criterion related. Content validation and criterion-related validation are the 2 strategies that are most directly applicable to the employment setting. A thumbnail sketch of each of these validation procedures is given below.

Content validation involves showing that the test represents an important sample of the job itself. A typing test for secretarial positions is an example of a test that is valid by virtue of its content. The person who does well on the typing test will have demonstrated proficiency in the typing aspect of the job. There is a direct connection between test content and job content.

Criterion-related validation involves administering the test to study subjects and subsequently obtaining suitable measures of job performance. The 2 pieces of data (test scores and job performance data) are then statistically correlated to determine the relationship between them. If the test is valid, the persons who score high on the test will tend to do better on the measure of job performance while those who do poorly on the test will tend to do correspondingly less well on the job. In criterion-related validation, job relatedness is established empirically by actually doing a study and observing how people with different test scores behave on the job. Standard statistical procedures are applied to the data to summarize the outcome of the study.

Q-40   Is it better to validate a test by the content or by the criterion-related procedure?

The 2 procedures are both professionally acceptable and each 1 is appropriate in the proper circumstances. The Supreme Court shares this point of view in a footnote to the *Washington v. Davis* (12 FEP 1415 (1976)) decision:

It appears beyond doubt by now that there is no single method for appropriately validating employment tests for their relationship to job performance. Professional standards developed by the American Psychological Association in its Standards for Educational and Psychological Tests and Manuals (1966) accept three basic methods of validation: "empirical" or "criterion" validity (demonstrated by identifying criteria that indicate successful job performance and then correlating test scores and the criteria so identified), "construct" validity (demonstrated by examinations structured to measure the degree to which job applicants have identifiable characteristics that have been demonstrated to be important in successful job performance), and "content" validity (demonstrated by tests whose content closely approximates tasks to be performed on the job by the applicant). These standards have been relied upon by the Equal Employment Opportunity Commission in fashioning its Guidelines on Employment Selection Procedures, 29 CFR pt. 1607, and have been judicially noted in cases where validation of employment tests have been in issue. (Citations deleted.)

Q-41 **If a test has been validated by the content procedure, is it necessary to confirm the results by means of a criterion-related study?**

A competently done content validation study is sufficient to establish the job relatedness of the test in question. One may wish to do a criterion-related study for the purpose, for example, of developing data for empirically based cutoff or passing scores. But this is a separate concern from the issue of validity. That is to say, it is one thing to say that policemen have to know English in order to perform their jobs competently (validity issue) and quite another to require that they know Shakespeare (cutoff score issue) (see *Q-21* and *Q-22*).

Q-42 **Do the concepts of differential validity and test fairness apply to content valid tests?**

It will be recalled that issues of differential validity and test fairness have to do with whether tests have the same meaning for different groups. A content valid test is a test that measures a representative sample of the job such that performance on the test directly translates to proficiency on the job. By definition, content valid tests are valid and fair to minority and nonminority groups.

Q-43 **Is it easier to perform a content validation study than a criterion-related study?**

Both validation procedures start out with a job analysis: a careful study of the job to determine what sorts of skills, abilities, and worker characteristics are required to competently perform the job. The next steps in both content and criterion-related studies is to select or develop the test that measures the relevant skill/ability requirements. Content validation stops at this point. In a criterion-related study, however, the investigator proceeds to develop a measure of job performance that will register individual differences in how well the job is done. Subsequently, the investigator administers the test to study subjects and obtains job performance criterion measures from those who are hired or promoted to the job in question. Statistical analyses are then carried out on the test and job performance data.

This telescoped account of how the 2 validation studies are conducted indicates that criterion-related validation is a more elaborate procedure than content validation. In this sense, it is easier to perform a content validation than a criterion-related validation study.

Q-44   Do the concepts of differential validity and test fairness apply to tests validated by the criterion-related method?

Yes. In order to develop information for differential validity and test fairness studies, it is necessary to conduct separate analyses for minority and nonminority groups (or males and females). This means that the study sample must include a sufficient number of minorities and nonminorities and validity data (test and job performance data) are generated for each group to permit the necessary comparisons. In practice, this is like doing the validation study twice.

Q-45   What if there are not enough minorities to do the separate analyses required by differential validity studies?

One of the requirements for doing a validation study is having a sample of study subjects that is sufficiently large to yield meaningful results. It used to be thought that 30 was the minimum number; more recent work indicates that this is probably on the low side. If there are not enough study subjects, a criterion-related validation study is said to be technically not feasible. If one has validity data on a sufficient number of nonminorities but the number of minorities is too small, a differential validity analysis is not technically feasible.

Q-46   Are there other prerequisites for doing a criterion-related validation study?

In addition to adequate sample size, the other technical requirement has to do with having a sufficient spread of scores on both the test and the criterion measure of job performance. It will be recalled that validation involves fundamentally a showing that those who score high on the test tend to do well on the job, while those who test out lower perform correspondingly poorer on the job. If there are virtually no individual differences on the job (as might happen when the better employees are promoted or leave for greener pastures and the poorer ones quit or are terminated, leaving a fairly homogeneous work group) or on the test (as might happen when only the top test scorers are included in the validation study sample), the test will show no apparent validity. The validities obtained under these conditions will be either low or nonexistent, reflecting the fact that the test is called upon to make very fine differentiations among members of a very select group. An everyday analogy might illustrate the point. Among very tall basketball players, height ceases to be associated with performance even though in the general population, it is the taller person who tends to be the better basketball player. There are, of course, exceptions that indicate less than perfect validity even for measures of physical attributes.

Reduced variability in either the test or the job performance measure leads to what is technically called restriction of range. Statistical procedures exist for correcting for restriction of range. The formulas estimate what the validities would have been if the full range of scores had been studied. If the restriction of range is too severe, a criterion-related validation study becomes technically infeasible.

A third condition that affects criterion-related validation studies has to do with the administrative aspects of managing the study. Criterion-related validation requires procedurally that the tests be administered in a standard fashion and that criterion measures of job performance be collected from study participants. If the time for completing the study drags on beyond a reasonable period (as might happen when the vacancies for the target job are few and far between), project continuity and management may be impaired. Furthermore, the research requirements of test validation represent an intrusion into the day-to-day operations of the enterprise. Protracted intrusions get to be bothersome.

Q-47   How long does it take to do a criterion-related validation study?

The answer depends on which of the strategies or study designs is used. In the concurrent strategy (also known as the present-employee method), job incumbents are tested and their test scores are correlated with a suitable measure of job performance. In the predictive design (also known as follow-up study), the tests are administered to job applicants and those who are hired are followed up on the job for the purpose of gathering the necessary job performance data. Invariably, the predictive design takes longer to complete since the development of the study sample is dependent on the number of job vacancies that develop, whereas in the concurrent type of study, the investigator has a "captive" audience of job incumbents. Counterbalancing the advantages of having a readily available pool of study subjects in a concurrent study are considerations that have to do with the extent to which incumbents are representative of the applicant population. Competently done, a concurrent study should yield results comparable to the predictive design.

Q-48   In view of the additional requirements associated with criterion-related validation, why aren't all employment tests validated by the content method?

There are procedural advantages to content validation. Not all tests, however, lend themselves to content validation. As a general rule, the more closely the test resembles the job (a typing test for a typist position, a road test for drivers, specific work experiences), the more likely it is that content validation is the appropriate method for showing the test's job relatedness. On the other hand, tests of intelligence, general ability, specific aptitudes, and other abstract attributes are most appropriately validated by means of the empirical and statistical procedures involved in criterion-related validation.

This discussion is not intended to suggest that content validation is a "piece of cake." Deciding which aspects of the job are to be represented in the test, sampling of the job domain that has been identified as relevant, and deciding on a passing score are considerations that must be added to the usual requirements (for example, clarity of the items) of developing a good, content valid instrument.

Q-49　What is involved in construct validation?

A construct is a hypothetical trait, attribute, or characteristic that gives unity and coherence to observable behavior. Anxiety, dominance, and aggression are illustrative examples. The process of construct validation involves a series of studies aimed at showing that the test measures the hypothetical attribute it purports to measure.

A simplified example involving the construct anxiety will illustrate what is involved in construct validation. Suppose a test is developed that is believed to measure the level of a person's anxiety. How might the necessary information be generated to validate the test? That is to say, how might it be shown that the test measures anxiety rather than some other trait such as intelligence or dominance? One would start out researching what is known about anxiety. It might be found, for example, that:

(a) Firstborns are more anxious than later borns. (The parents' inexperience in starting a family, the initial period of adjustment and settling down after the honeymoon, combined with living up to the expectations of each other's in-laws may be cited as generating anxiety among the parents-to-be and that this anxiety is passed on to the children with the firstborn taking the major share.)

(b) Drug X has the effect of heightening anxiety. (The chemical action of Drug X on the appropriate section of the body is cited as responsible for the drug's effect.)

(c) Neurotics are more anxious than normals. (A high level of anxiety is 1 of the classic symptoms of neurosis.)

A series of studies would then be set up that might include:

(a) giving the test of anxiety to a group of firstborns and their later-born siblings;

(b) giving the test to subjects who have been administered Drug X and to a control group that has been administered some innocuous placebo, such as saline;

(c) administering the test to a group of study subjects who are known to be neurotics and to a control group classified as "normal."

If the test measures the construct anxiety, it should be found that firstborns score higher on the test than their later-born brothers or sisters; that the group administered Drug X scores higher on the test than the control group; and that neurotics score higher on the test than normal study subjects. In short, if the test measures anxiety, it should be expected that people who score high on the test will behave the way that anxious people behave.

The steps taken to research the literature for what is known about the construct (thereby permitting development of a series of predictions) and the studies performed to test these predictions illustrate what is involved in construct validation. It is not difficult to see that the steps involved in construct validation resemble the steps involved in developing and testing a theory.

Q-50 Construct validation seems like a highly involved process. Is it ever used in the employment setting?

In the simplified example involving anxiety, an attempt was made to show that construct validation represents more than a 1-shot study. It is a complex strategy for showing that a test measures what it claims to measure. Most frequently used in the clinical setting where constructs such as dominance, aggression, and anxiety are driving considerations, the application of construct validation as a strategy for demonstrating the job relatedness of employment tests has been limited. It is possible that construct validation of employment tests may involve a combination of content and criterion-related studies—a prospect that would render construct validation technically not feasible for all but the largest employers.

Q-51 Suppose a company hires Joe on the basis of his high scores on a validated pre-employment test. Joe, however, does not work out on the job. What does this say about the validity of the test?

Several points need to be made in response to this question:

1. Establishing the validity of a test (or its lack of validity, for that matter) requires careful study, frequently involving the participation of a number of study subjects. One early rule of thumb provided that 30 study subjects were the minimum required for a criterion-related validation study. Later work indicated that the threshold requirement of 30 was on the low side. The point to be made is that the behavior of 1 person provides very little information about the validity of

a test. Furthermore, no employment test is perfectly valid and there will be occasional "misses"—persons who test high but do not perform well on the job and those whose low test performance underpredicts their actual job performance. It is frequently these persons who catch the eye; those who contribute to test validity by behaving on the job in accordance with what their test scores indicate are playing by the rules and are therefore not as noticeable as the exceptions.

2. Job performance is multidimensional: There is more to success on the job than what an aptitude test measures. A test of ability will rarely identify those persons who can competently perform the job but who are not motivated to do their best for reasons that may have to do with boredom, lack of interest, or resentment of company practices.

3. Reports of discrepancies between test performance and job performance frequently occur after the test has been validated and is on-line. As noted above, the exceptions support the rule; they also attract attention. If, however, the incidence of lowered job performance among presumably test-qualified workers persists or reaches proportions that are practically significant, it may be necessary to review the situation. The review may show that substantive changes in the job have eroded the validity and usefulness of the test or the review may point to serious breach in test security as the causative agent.

To summarize, it is not likely that a testing program can be feasibly set up that captures all the determinants of job success; those that can be practicably captured are measured with some margin of error (that is, with less than perfect validity). Intimations that the test does not seem to be working, even when they are based on the casual observation of line supervisors, should be regarded as warning signals. Vigilance for the full spectrum of contributing factors, rather than panic over the sudden loss of validity, is the appropriate response.

Q–52   What is face validity?

The concept of face validity has to do with whether a particular test appears reasonable and valid to examinees who take it, to test administrators who give the test, and to other persons with limited professional training who use test results in the decision-making process. Strictly speaking, face validity is not a technical requirement but is considered important for a testing program's acceptance and long-term viability. A test containing questions that are trivial or frivolous lends itself to ridicule and may lead examinees to take it less seriously than they should. An examinee who is disqualified by virtue of failing to meet test standards can be expected to dispute vigorously the relevance of a test weighted down by trivial items. In sum, tests that appear reasonable and make sense on their face go a long way toward enhancing the integrity of a valid testing program.

Q-53 *Is face validity important for cosmetic reasons?*

A testing program is more than just a standardized exercise for measuring job qualifications. It is also a social relationship between the test-using employer and its potential workforce with important public relations implications for the company and its image. In today's environment, employment testing is also a legal transaction in which examinees represent potential plaintiffs in employment discrimination lawsuits. In this context, a test that is face valid decreases the probability of provoking serious legal challenges while the test's technical validity speaks to the probability of successfully defending against the challenge. The 2 concepts may be analogously compared with how frequently one has to go to war and how one is likely to fare after the forces are engaged. Although none of the foregoing considerations is a technical requirement of a sound testing program, they can hardly be termed cosmetic reasons for face valid, ostensibly reasonable instruments of job qualifications.

Q-54 *Can validity be established by visual inspection of the items comprising the test?*

No. Establishing the job relatedness of a test requires a careful study that involves either showing that the test representatively samples important aspects of the job (content validation) or that performance on the test is significantly correlated with performance on the job (criterion-related validation). These procedures are rigorous and represent the professionally acceptable ways of validating a test. Visual inspection of the items for their apparent correspondence with job performance would be aimed at face validity. As *Q-53* notes, face validity is important but it is not a sufficient basis for establishing the job relatedness of tests.

To answer the question another way, if test validity were established visually, a given test would have as many validities as there are viewers and the fundamental soundness of a testing program would reside in the eye of the beholder.

Q-55 *What is the difference between the concept of job relatedness and validity?*

The 2 concepts are very similar: A valid test is one that measures skills, abilities, and characteristics demonstrably related to the job in question such that those who score high on the test have a higher probability of being better on the job than those with lower test scores.

There are, however, several dimensions on which the 2 concepts differ:

1. The concept of job relatedness is broader than the concept of validity. That is to say, validation is only 1 way of showing job relatedness. Bona fide occupational

qualifications (BFOQ) and bona fide seniority systems represent ways of demonstrating the business necessity/job relatedness of challenged practices for which validity data are either unavailable (because they do not exist) or infeasible (for such technical reasons as excessive restriction of range, criterion unreliability, or inadequate sample size) to develop. Where employment tests are concerned, however, validation is the most common method of demonstrating job relatedness.

2. Job relatedness has more of a legal character, whereas the concept of validity has more of a psychological ring. An employment test is considered to be validated when the supporting study is conducted in accordance with professional standards (for example, American Psychological Association Standards for Educational and Psychological Tests and Manuals). The same study may be found wanting by a court of law for reasons that may have to do with the failure of the study to comply with specific provisions in the *Uniform Guidelines on Employee Selection Procedures*. This anomalous situation arises to the extent that professional standards and federal testing guidelines contain nonidentical provisions and to the extent that arbiters rely on the latter to evaluate the job relatedness of challenged procedures.

3. A consideration related to number 2 above has to do with the stimulus that triggers the showing of job relatedness or validity. It will be recalled that the legal requirement for a showing of job relatedness arises after the complaining party makes out a prima facie case of discrimination by showing, for example, that the selection procedures in question has a substantial adverse impact. This is generally the framework for allocating the order and burden of proof in a legal proceeding (see *Q–85*). In other words, if a selection device such as a test has no adverse impact, there is no legal requirement to show that it is job related. It has been facetiously observed that where a test has no adverse impact, it may be used for good reasons, for bad reasons, or for no reason. It has been argued that the use of validated selection procedures is a prudent business practice designed to ensure that selection decisions are made on the basis of job-relevant standards. Hence, even though the legal framework imposes no obligation on the test user to validate his selection procedure for job relatedness when there is no adverse impact, it makes good business sense to select employees on the basis of valid, job-relevant qualifications. If the validity data that are generated in the course of establishing job relevant standards also can be used to show job relatedness in the event that the selection procedure is legally assailed, one will have killed 2 birds with 1 stone.

All of the foregoing is another way of saying that the threat of litigation should focus, not distort, one's priorities with respect to the use of tests to advance what is good for the business. In a legal proceeding, job relatedness is the defendant's burden; in everyday operations, validity is the test user's bottom line for determining whether a particular selection procedure is doing its job. Validating tests, in short, makes good business and legal sense.

Q-56   How are the outcomes of validation studies reported?

The results of validation studies are generally reported in 2 formats that differ in the amount of detail with which the information is presented.

Technical reports describe study procedures and study outcomes in sufficient detail to permit the professional reader to arrive at an independent judgment of the soundness of the procedures used and of the extent to which the conclusions and interpretations are justified by the data. Technical reports are written using the rule of thumb that another professional should be able to replicate or reconstruct the essential steps in the study from the description provided by the report.

Sometimes, validation studies are published in refereed technical journals, such as the *Journal of Applied Psychology*. Studies that are so published are deemed by a panel of experts to be of such exemplary caliber that they deserve wider dissemination to the professional audience of the particular journal. The journal version of a validation study is typically condensed to meet criteria of conciseness and parsimony. The criteria of conciseness and parsimony come close to what is colloquially known as "space limitations."

In addition to technical reports, validation studies are also written in what may be called an administrative format for use by company or client personnel. A manual for administering, scoring, and interpreting the recommended operational test or test battery may be included. Occasionally, executive summaries are also provided.

The different formats for reporting the outcome of validation studies represent different versions of the same story written to satisfy different audiences and different criteria. To a professional audience, test validity may be appropriately expressed as a correlation coefficient, while to personnel managers and company executives, the same information may be best conveyed by means of graphical expectancy charts. Similarly, a field investigator for a state agency looking into a charge of employment discrimination may be satisfied with an executive summary, while in a more formal legal proceeding, a report written to conform to the documentation requirements of the *Uniform Guidelines on Employee Selection Procedures* may be indicated. To resort to an overworked analogy: Sometimes knowing the time of day is all that one needs; at other times, detailed and explicit directions for making a clock are indicated.

Q-57   How is validity different from the concept of reliability?

The concept of reliability has to do with the notion of precision or consistency of measurement, while the concept of validity has to do with the relevance of what is measured. A test of mechanical comprehension would be reliable if examinees tended to get about the same test scores when tested

Users may, under certain circumstances, support the use of selection procedures by validity studies conducted by other users or conducted by test publishers or distributors and described in test manuals. While publishers of selection procedures have a professional obligation to provide evidence of validity which meets generally accepted professional standards (see section 5c above), users are cautioned that they are responsible for compliance with these guidelines. Accordingly, users seeking to obtain selection procedures from publishers and distributors should be careful to determine that, in the event the user becomes subject to the validity requirements of these guidelines, the necessary information to support validity has been determined and will be made available to the user.

   B. Use of criterion-related evidence from other sources.
Criterion-related validity studies conducted by one test user, or described in test manuals and the professional literature, will be considered acceptable for use by another when the following conditions are met:

   (1) Validity evidence. Evidence from the available studies meeting the standards of section 14B below clearly demonstrates that the selection procedure is valid;

   (2) Job similarity. The incumbents in the user's job and the incumbents in the job or group of jobs on which the validity was conducted perform substantially the same major work behaviors, as shown by appropriate job analyses both on the job or group of jobs on which the validity study was performed and on the job for which the selection procedure is to be used; and

   (3) Fairness evidence. The studies include a study of test fairness for each race, sex, and ethnic group which constitutes a significant factor in the borrower user's relevant labor market for the job or jobs in question. If the studies under consideration satisfy (1) and (2) above but do not contain an investigation of test fairness, and it is technically not feasible for the borrowing user to conduct an internal study of test fairness, the borrowing user may utilize the study until studies conducted elsewhere meeting the requirements of these guidelines show test unfairness, or until such time as it becomes technically feasible to conduct an internal study of test fairness and the results of that study can be acted upon. Users obtaining selection procedures from publishers should consider, as one factor in the decision to purchase a particular selection procedure, the availability of evidence concerning test fairness.

   C. Validity evidence from multiunit study.
If validity evidence from a study covering more than one unit within one organization satisfies the requirements of section 14B below, evidence of validity specific to each unit will not be required unless there are variables which are likely to affect validity significantly.

   D. Other significant variables.
If there are variables in the other studies which are likely to affect validity significantly, the user may not rely upon such studies, but will be expected either to conduct an internal study or to comply with section 6 above.

Q-59 How is test validity expressed or reported?

   The observed relationship between performance on the test and perfor- mance on a criterion of job performance is usually expressed as a correlation coefficient. The correlation coefficient, designated by the small letter r, is a statistical index for summarizing the relationship between 2 variables in a single number that ranges in value from 0 (indicative of no relationship) to 1.00 (indicative of a perfect relationship). The variables of interest in a validation study are the scores on the test and scores on the measure of job performance. The higher the absolute value of r, the stronger is the relationship and the greater is the accuracy of predicting job performance from test performance.

The correlation coefficient has 2 components: an absolute value that indicates the magnitude of the relationship and a positive or negative sign that indicates the direction (direct or inverse) of the relationship. Personnel tests with negative validities (ability tests that are negatively correlated with job performance) are seldom used operationally in the employment setting for it would indicate that the lower test performers tend to be the better workers—a circumstance that, if widely publicized, may encourage applicants to fake their scores downward in order to enhance their prospects of being hired.

Sometimes it is useful to present the outcome of a validation study graphically by means of what are known as expectancy charts. An expectancy chart is a graphical representation of what job performance outcomes can be expected from hiring people scoring at various score ranges on the test. There are 2 types of expectancy charts: individual and institutional. The difference between the 2 is depicted in Figures 1 and 2 and discussed in the accompanying text.

- In this hypothetical example, the test distribution has been broken down into 5 groups or categories (column 2) and the test score ranges associated with each group are shown (column 1). Thus, the top 20% of the examinees obtained test scores of 59 or higher while the bottom 20% of the group scored below 41 on the test.

- Suppose a satisfactory employee is defined as one who completes so many widgets per hour. Within each of the 5 test categories, the number meeting the criterion we set up of producing the desired number of widgets per hour is counted off and expressed as a percentage of the individuals in the particular test category. The top bar shows that of the top 20% test scores (or, alternatively, among those who score 59 or better on the test) two-thirds or 67% would turn out to be satisfactory on the job. At the other extreme, among the bottom 20% test scorers, only 33% are satisfactory on the job. The other bars are similarly interpreted.

- The chart graphically portrays the probability of being satisfactory on the job associated with different test score ranges. Thus, the top 20% of the examinees have twice as many chances of being satisfactory job performers as those who score in the bottom 20% of the test distribution.

- Note the linear trend of the relationship between test performance and job performance: The higher the test score, the better the odds of working out satisfactorily on the job.

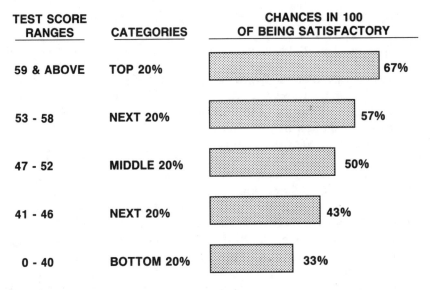

Figure 1
Individual Expectancy Chart (Hypothetical)

• The actuarial nature of predicting job performance from test score data is also
evident: Not everyone who scores in the highest test bracket is a satisfactory job
performer but it is clear that proportionately more of the satisfactory job
performers come from higher test performers.

   The institutional expectancy chart in Figure 2 utilizes test score categories
that are cumulative: top 20%, top 40%, top 60%, and so on. Except for the
top bar, each succeeding category includes the data from the preceding
categories. The second bar, for example, consists of the data from the top
20% as well as the data from the next 20% of test scorers—or from the top
40%. Figure 2 shows that as more of the lower test scoring categories are
included, the quality of the selectees gets proportionately "diluted" and the
proportion of satisfactory workers declines.

   The last bar in Figure 2 shows that if all the examinees were hired or were
selected purely at random without the use of the test, 50% of the selectees
would be satisfactory on the job. This figure is called the base rate. The
practical usefulness of a test is evaluated by comparing the degree of
improvement over the base rate that results from using the test to select
employees. Figure 2 shows that if the top 40% of the test scorers were
selected (of whom 62% would be satisfactory on the job), the improvement
over the base rate is 12%.

   Institutional expectancy charts are useful not only for communicating the
results of a validation study but also for assessing the long-term impact of

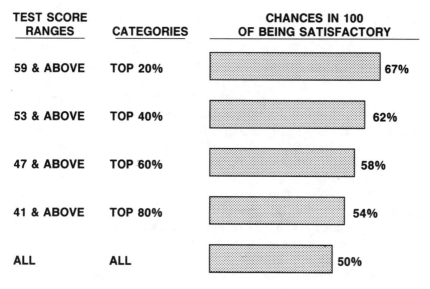

TEST SCORE RANGES	CATEGORIES	CHANCES IN 100 OF BEING SATISFACTORY
59 & ABOVE	TOP 20%	67%
53 & ABOVE	TOP 40%	62%
47 & ABOVE	TOP 60%	58%
41 & ABOVE	TOP 80%	54%
ALL	ALL	50%

Figure 2
Institutional Expectancy Chart (Hypothetical)

particular test usage strategies in terms of gains over the base rate and in terms of the selection ratio (the proportion meeting a given test standard among applicants in the reference population).

Q-60 *Is a test with a validity of .30 better than a test with a validity of .35?*

The answer depends on a number of factors that are important in evaluating an obtained validity coefficient. For purposes of this discussion, it will be assumed that the validation studies for the 2 tests in question were conducted competently and that the studies are comparable in other respects save for the differences in the levels of validities obtained. The question would then reduce to how one interprets and assesses study outcomes. That is to say, the answer responds to the question of how one interprets a validity coefficient of .30 or .35, rather than to the question of what makes 1 validation study better than another.

Statistical significance. Is the obtained relationship between test performance and job performance, reflected in the validity coefficient, sufficiently strong to warrant the conclusion that the results most probably represent a bona fide state of affairs rather than a fluke occurrence? Could the observed correlation coefficients have been due to chance? Could the obtained validities have arisen through chance fluctuations of sampling from a true correlation of 0? Are the study results, in brief, statistically significant?

The concept of statistical significance deals with the probability of obtaining certain results from a sample (for example, the particular sample of study subjects participating in the validation effort) based on characteristics of the larger population from which the sample was drawn and to which generalizations are to be made (for example, the population of applicants for the job in question). Most people can intuitively see that sample results mirror the population state of affairs. If, for example, there is no relationship between test performance and job performance in the population, it would not be surprising if a validation study utilizing a sample drawn from that population yielded test validities in the neighborhood of 0. Similarly, one is more likely to observe validities of .30 or higher in samples drawn from populations in which there is a relationship between test performance and job performance. It is not difficult to see, on an intuitive basis, that test validities observed in study samples become more or less probable depending on the true state of affairs in the population. What may not be intuitively obvious is that even under conditions of 0 validity in the population, validities obtained from sample results could—purely by chance—reach levels of .30 or better.

Inferential statistics provide us with decision rules for judging whether a particular value of a validity coefficient is more likely to have come from a population in which higher test scorers are not better job performers than low test scorers (0 validity) or from a population in which test performance is a bona fide determinant of job performance. A validity coefficient is said to be statistically significant if it reaches levels that make us confident in concluding that there is indeed a genuine relationship between scores on the test and performance on the job. The convention is to report the 1% (designated $p < .01$) and the 5% ($p < .05$) levels of statistical significance or *alpha levels*. In the context of the present discussion, a test that is valid at the 1% level of significance indicates that the strength of the relationship between test performance and job performance observed in the sample is such that the chances are only 1 in 100 that the observed findings are a fluke. Put another way and in question form: What is the probability of obtaining a correlation as high as the one we observed in our sample if there is no relationship between the test and the criterion of job performance in the larger population to which generalizations are to be made? The odds are 1 in 20 (at the 5% level of significance) or 1 in 100 (at the 1% level of significance). Since these odds are so small, it can be concluded that in the population of job candidates from which the sample was drawn, higher test scorers tend to be better job performers than lower test scorers. That is to say, the test is indeed valid.

Statistical significance is a threshold requirement for tests that are to be used in the employment setting. More accurately, the levels of test validities must reach or exceed critical values required for statistical significance. Reason? If the relationship is a chance phenomenon and there is really no correlation between test performance and job performance, there would be little point in using the test in the employment process since the higher test scorer would not be any more likely to do well on the job than his lower test scoring counterpart. Use of the invalid test in the hiring process would represent an unnecessary hurdle for all applicants, a screening device with no business justification. Furthermore, where the invalid test in question is one in which minorities score lower than nonminorities, its use in hiring becomes a greater source of irrelevant difficulty for minority applicants, adversely affecting their chances of employment and exposing the test-using employer to unfair discrimination lawsuits.

Variance accounted for. Squaring the validity coefficient tells us what proportion of the variation in job performance is attributable to the test. This is the variance-accounted-for interpretation: A test with a validity of .30 accounts for or "explains" 9% of the individual differences in job performance, leaving 91% of the variation unaccounted for. This particular interpretation of test validity ascertains the extent to which variation in job performance can be explained by or attributed to differences in test performance. Since few employment tests reach validity levels of .50, the maximum variance that can be explained is no more than 25%—nothing to write home about. The variance-accounted-for interpretation of validity does not paint a very rosy picture of employment tests because the interpretation is unduly stringent (see *Q-62*).

Practical utility. The preceding 2 interpretations of test validity are statistical in nature. Because they are directed at the numbers, they have a cold, laboratory-like quality. They are insensitive to contextual variations, retaining their correctness under adverse labor market conditions as well as in situations where the supply of applicants exceeds the demand.

There are a number of interpretations that recognize that the practical usefulness of a test depends on the influence of situational factors. For convenience, these alternative explanations are referred to collectively as practical utility interpretations. Although the formulations vary somewhat, the principal theme is the same: The statistical properties of a test (for example, validity or level of statistical significance) do not adequately describe the practical gains that are realized when a test is used in particular settings. Two situational variables are discussed below:

Selection Ratio. The selection ratio is defined as the number of hires relative to the number of applicants. A selection ratio of 1.00 indicates that the number of available applicants is equal to the number of openings. Smaller selection ratios provide the employer with more room to select the best qualified.

Reference to the expectancy chart in Figure 2 (see *Q-59*) shows how the selection ratio affects the usefulness of a test. The top bar represents a selection ratio of .20: Only the top 20% of the examinees are hired. Among this group, 67% turn out to be satisfactory job performers. As the selection ratio increases (for example, where 8 out of 10 examinees are selected), the gains in criterion performance diminish.

To summarize, under adverse labor market conditions when the employer is put in the posture of hiring virtually everyone who applies, a test with the highest validity will not be useful in improving the quality of the intake. With improved selection ratios that permit the employer to "skim the cream," a test with modest validity can contribute substantially to the practical effectiveness of selection.

Base Rate. Base rate is the term that describes the relative incidence of a given behavior in the population. In a selection scenario, the behavior of interest is satisfactory job performance and base rate refers to the proportion of satistactory employees selected without the test. If the base rate is very high (indicating that virtually everyone can perform the job satisfactorily or that existing nontest selection criteria are working well), there would hardly be any point to installing a testing program, however high the test validities. On the other hand, if the job is such that only a very small fraction of the population can be successful, the massive testing that is required to identify that small fraction may render testing economically infeasible. Most business situations fall between the 2 extremes.

The base rate provides a benchmark for gauging the usefulness of a test. Reference is made again to the institutional expectancy chart in Figure 2 (see *Q-59*) where it is noted that the base rate is 50%. When the selection ratio is .20, the improvement over the base rate is 17% (67% minus 50%). It might be noted here that the validity of the test used to generate the expectancy chart in Figure 2 is approximately .30. The improvement attributable to the use of the test is referred to as the test's incremental validity. Incremental validity decreases as the selection ratio increases. At a selection ratio of .60, incremental validity is 8% (58% minus 50%).

Practical utility interpretations call attention to 3 key factors that have an impact on bottom-line results associated with test usage:

- Validity: The higher the validity coefficient, the more accurate is the prediction of job performance from test performance. When the validity is 0, no improvement over the base rate occurs at any selection ratio.

- Selection ratio: The number of hires relative to the number of applicants determines how selective the employer can be under prevailing labor market conditions. When the selection ratio is 1.00 and the employer must hire every available applicant, no gains over the base rate will be realized with tests of any validity level. As the selection ratio improves, tests with modest validities become practically useful.

- Base rate: The proportion of satisfactory employees in the reference population is a good indicator of how well existing selection devices (whose validities may be unstudied), exclusive of the test under consideration, are working. The utility of a test depends on the extent to which its use improves the caliber of selectees beyond the benchmark figures provided by the base rate.

The best combination consists of a moderate base rate coupled with high validities and low selection ratios: Highest gains are realized when the test user is able to select the highest scoring persons on a test that measures applicant characteristics maximally relevant to the job in question. To put it another way, the batting average would be no better than the base rate when test validity is 0 (selection is based on a test that does not measure bona fide job requirements) or when the selection ratio is 1.00 (everyone who is called is chosen).

Most test users are faced with situations that depart in varying degrees from the optimal mix of base rate, validity, and selection ratio. Taylor-Russell (1939) tables are available that show the improvement over varying base rates associated with different combinations of selection ratio and validity. What 1 table might look like is shown in Table 1.

Table 1
Selected Entries from Taylor-Russell Tables (base rate = .60)

	Selection Ratio			
	.10	.20	.50	.90
Validity				
.00	.60	.60	.60	.60
.20	.73	.71	.66	.62
.30	.79	.76	.69	.62
.40	.85	.81	.73	.63
.60	.94	.90	.80	.65
.80	.99	.98	.88	.66

- When validity is 0, no improvement over the base rate occurs at all selection ratios: The top test scorers are not any more likely to be better job performers than the low test scorers.
- If virtually everyone is selected (selection ratio of .90), even a test with validity of .80 yields an increase of only 6% over the base rate.
- If only the top 10% of test scorers are selected, a test with a validity of .40 will raise the percentage of satisfactory job performers from .60 to .85.

Two caveats: First, the Taylor-Russell tables represent but 1 of several conceptualizations that take into account the influence of nonstatistical factors on test usage. Taylor-Russell tables were selected to illustrate the impact of contextual variables on a test's incremental validity. Similar thinking is discernible in the works to H. Brogden (1946), L. Cronbach and G. Gleser (1965), and J. Naylor and L. Shine (1965). The message is fairly consistent: Practical utility interpretations present a more encouraging picture of employment tests than the variance-accounted-for interpretation. Second, this discussion has ignored the cost of testing—the cost of test materials, test administration, test scoring, and test interpretation. For most paper-and-pencil, group-administered tests of ability, these costs are not high. Where more complicated procedures are involved (for example, assessment center techniques in which the job candidate goes through a series of role-playing exercises and where a team of assessors is needed to administer the exercises or to "score" the candidate's performance), the costs of processing an applicant can be substantial. Striving for too low a selection ratio may become economically prohibitive and the employer may have to settle for something short of the optimal or consider a sequential strategy in which a paper-and-pencil test is used as a front-end screen to the assessment process.

A summarizing statement: The actual gains from using a test reflect the interplay of the statistical (validity) and the situational (base rate, selection ratio), balanced by the cost of testing. The level of test validity, represented by the correlation coefficient or its square, is only 1 part of a bigger picture.

Q-61   Is the message from the Taylor-Russell tables that one could maximize selection ratios rather than test validities?

The Taylor-Russell tables are not intended to suggest that enhanced selection ratios are a substitute for test validity. As discussed in *Q-63*, the validity ceiling for employment tests is not very high—in the neighborhood of .50—for reasons that are given in *Q-64*. Given this state of affairs, the Taylor-Russell tables indicate that enlarging the pool of applicants from which to identify the highest test scorers can lead to material payoffs on the job.

There are circumstances that limit the extent to which selection ratios can be maximized in practice. Cost of testing is 1 such constraint; the need to fill personnel requisitions in a timely fashion is another. Other considerations include the criticality of the job being filled, the relative risks associated with hiring someone who turns out to be unsuccessful on the job (*false positives,* persons whose high test performance falsely predicts their low job behavior) vis-à-vis the risks of rejecting someone who would have been a crackerjack on the job (*false negatives*), the adequacy of training programs to alleviate erroneous hiring decisions, and the efficacy of performance appraisal systems for identifying employees in need of developmental or outplacement treatment.

The message from the Taylor-Russell tables ought to be that tests are seldom used *in vacuo*. In the real world, test validity gets caught up in the dynamic stream of situational variables and the fluid churn of organizational expediencies.

Q-62 Is the variance-accounted-for interpretation of test validity a correct interpretation?

Yes. Squaring the validity coefficient does tell what proportion of the individual differences in the criterion of job performance is accounted for by individual differences in test performance. The mathematical accuracy of this particular interpretation tends to mask the situationally determined practical gains associated with specific test usages. In addition, the following consequences flow from the variance-accounted-for interpretation:

1. A test with a validity of $+.30$ would account for the same amount of variance as a test with a validity of $-.30$, since squaring a number has the effect of ignoring its sign, positive or negative. By the variance-accounted-for interpretation, a test with negative validity is just as useful as a test with positive validity. As observed in *Q-59*, the direction of the relationship between test performance and job performance is important: Acting on the results of a test with negative validity would, if widely known, lead applicants to fake their scores downward in order to increase their prospects of being selected.

2. The variance-accounted-for interpretation requires that the test be able to predict a person's precise standing on the criterion of job performance. If a person's actual job performance turns out to be better than what his test scores indicate, this "error" in prediction is counted against the test. Very few, if any, selection situations call for this degree of precision. In general, most employers are interested in tests that can predict with some degree of accuracy whether Joe or Jack will come up to some level of performance that separates the winners from the losers. An examinee's likely standing on broad categories of performance rather than his precise job performance is what people have in mind when they wonder whether "Joe will do all right" or whether "Jack will work out on the job" or whether either "will cut the mustard."

   In addition, there are certain errors of prediction that do not make a practical difference. Suppose, for example, that Joe and Jack are both satisfactory workers and both are hired because they passed the employment test. It matters little whether Joe scored higher on the test than Jack while in job performance, Jack is better than Joe. Even though the difference in job performance (Jack is better than Joe) was not "accounted for" by their comparative test performance (where Joe scored higher than Jack), the statistical error is not practically important. The important thing is that both applicants met the standards on the test and they both met the standards on the job. Certain errors of prediction are irrelevant to the selection situation—something that the variance-accounted-for interpretation fails to take into account.

As a general rule, the variance-accounted-for interpretation will tend to paint a rather discouraging picture of employment tests. In employment discrimination lawsuits in which testing has been an issue, it is not uncommon to find the expert witness for the plaintiff urge the variance-accounted-for interpretation in order to discredit the test in question. Expressions such as *"the glass is half empty or half full"* and *"cursing the darkness or lighting a candle''* can be used to distinguish between the variance-accounted-for and practical utility interpretations of test validity.

Q-63 What is the average validity of employment tests?

E. Ghiselli (1966) compiled an extensive summary of validation studies involving different aptitude tests for different occupations and for different criterion measures. Ghiselli's survey shows that the average validity of employment tests against proficiency criteria (that is, to predict actual job behavior) is .20 and the average validity against training criteria (to predict performance in training) is .30. It should be noted that these figures are average figures, reflecting the outcome of many studies that vary in quality. Furthermore, the data are for individual tests rather than for test batteries. The validity of tests used in combination would be higher. Even so, the reported validities are not impressive. By the variance-accounted-for interpretation of test validity, employment tests account for an average of 4% and 9% of individual differences in job and training performance, respectively.

Q-64 Why are test validities not any higher than those reported by Ghiselli?

For at least the following reasons:

1. Performance on the job—the criterion that employment tests aim to predict—is determined by a host of factors that fall roughly into 2 categories: those that are within the worker's control and those that are not. Among the former are goal-directed efforts mediated by ability (*can do*) and motivational (*will do*) characteristics of the job holder. Individual differences in the outcome of these efforts are likely to correlate with individual differences in test performance, thereby contributing to the test's validity. The factors that lie outside of the incumbent's control but that affect his job performance include the quality of supervision, peer group pressure to restrict productivity, the availability of tools, quality of machines, working conditions, and plain luck. There may be others. Tests will seldom correlate with aspects of job performance that are determined by factors outside of the employee's control. Most gamblers discover that it is very difficult and costly to predict outcomes that are due to chance. In the dynamic interaction between the *"sweat of one's brow"* and *"being in the right place at the right time,"* factors that define job success, only the ability component lends itself to prediction by the typical paper-and-pencil employment test.

2. The criterion measures used in validating tests are imperfect measures of job success. At some level of abstraction, the true worth of an employee consists of his career contributions to the attainment of organizational objectives. This level of organizational accomplishment, summed over many assignments and opportuni-

ties, defines the sort of criterion of job behavior that one would like employment tests to be able to predict. Unable to capture this ultimate criterion, one resorts to such proxies as supervisory testimonials registered in rating scales of 1 sort or another or to conveniently accessible measures such as records of turnover, length of service, absenteeism, and tardiness that are routinely maintained for administrative purposes rather than to serve as criteria for validation research.

3. Even if all the determinants of job success were known, psychometric and practical considerations would prevent developing the sort of test battery that would incorporate all the factors that lead to occupational success. Costs of testing—materials, administration, space and scheduling requirements, and similar mundane considerations—place a limit on the length of a testing session and on the number of tests that can practically be included in a test battery. Measures of the *"will do"* correlates of job performance, such as motivational, interpersonal, and other affective inventories, are beset with psychometric problems of the sort that render them virtually unsuitable for employment selection purposes except in special circumstances (see *Q-9*). Employment tests used in the hiring process capture but a small segment of what it takes to succeed.

4. A number of statistical artifacts makes it difficult for test validities to show their true colors. The artifacts include unreliability and restriction of range in either the test, the criterion of job performance, or both. Furthermore, where supervisory judgments are used, rater tendencies (such as the tendency to assign mostly favorable performance ratings across performance dimensions or across people) obscure individual differences and lead to reduced validities.

To summarize by resorting to an analogy: Validating an employment test is much like trying to shoot the elusive target called job success with a short burst of gunfire provided by employment tests under the obscuring haze of statistical artifacts. Small wonder we hit the target about 9% of the time.

Q-65 What implications flow from Ghiselli's review of test validities?

The general message is simply that tests are fallible devices and predictions based on test scores are subject to error. This does not mean that tests should be banned; it does mean that test data should be used with care.

There is general professional consensus with the notion that a person's test performance represents but 1 piece of information in determining his overall suitability as a job candidate. There are other sources of pertinent data (for example, interview, reference checks) that can be used to yield a whole person view of the applicant. To be sure, strict adherence to established test standards makes for greater standardization and uniform treatment of all examinees. There is a difference, however, between wooden application and disciplined flexibility; the former represents mindless abdication of business judgment while the latter reflects the responsible exercise of managerial discretion.

Exclusive reliance on test performance without regard to possible extenuating or compensatory factors reinforces the thinking noted in the introductory section—something is wrong with a society in which one's livelihood or career depends on a single number, his test score.

Q–66   *Are employment tests biased against minorities?*

The answer depends on how one defines test bias. By the prevailing definition of test bias, employment tests are not biased against minorities. If anything, the evidence suggests that employment tests tend to give minority job applicants a slight edge over their white counterparts. The answer may become clearer if we put it in historical perspective.

Early definition of test bias centered on the content of the tests. Since the tests were developed by members of the majority group (that is, middle class whites) and the test questions were about the dominant culture, the tests were culture-bound and therefore unfair to members of minority groups. Visual inspection of test items and observed differences in test performance between minority and nonminority examinee groups were sufficient to establish test bias by this definition. The remedy was straightforward: Develop tests that would minimize or reduce the differences between groups by asking questions, for example, that were either equally familiar or equally unfamiliar to minorities and nonminorities. Such tests were called "culture-fair" or "culture-free." Nonverbal and abstract reasoning tests were proposed as examples.

The next wave of inquiry about test bias raised questions that have to do with whether tests have the same meaning for minorities and nonminorities. Is the test that "works" for 1 group also applicable to the other group? Is the test an appropriate measure of job qualifications for whites but not for blacks, and vice versa? These questions clearly go beyond the actual content of the test. The questions imply that if minorities as a group score lower on a test than their nonminority counterparts, the significance of these group differences in test performance must be studied.

Whether tests behave differently (that is, have different meanings) for minorities and nonminorities has been evaluated principally in 2 ways: by means of studies that involve relating the test scores of each group separately to such outcomes as performance in school, in training, or on the job (these studies are collectively called studies of differential validity) and by means of analyses that ascertain the effects of using test scores operationally to arrive at accept/reject decisions affecting minority and non-minority job candidates (the different formulations are referred to as alternative models of test fairness).

Differential validity issues deal with the question of whether the pattern of relationships between test performance and job performance is the same for minorities and nonminorities. Is the test that is valid and job related for whites also similarly valid for blacks? Test fairness issues, on the other hand, address the consequences of using test scores to determine who gets hired (or promoted) and who does not. Do job candidates, black or white, who have the same probability of successfully performing the job also have the same probability of being selected for the job? Stated differently, validity is a characteristic of the test as a measuring device; fairness is a property of how a test, as a personnel decision tool, is used in particular employment contexts. In more technical language, differential validity is concerned with group differences in validity coefficients, while test fairness is concerned with group differences in prediction systems.

The evidence is fairly strong that occupational tests of the type commonly used in personnel settings are appropriate for use with minorities and nonminorities alike. In more specific terms, with respect to the question of differential validity, the evidence is very strong that a test that is valid for whites will also be valid and to the same extent as for blacks. With respect to the question of test fairness, the studies indicate that the job performance of blacks tends to be slightly overpredicted (not underpredicted, as originally hypothesized) by tests. By the prevailing definition of test fairness (Cleary's regression model), which is concerned with the accuracy of prediction, employment tests tend to be positively biased in favor of minorities. (If a person's job performance were underpredicted by the test, he would not be selected by virtue of his low test score even though he would have been successful on the job. Conversely, overprediction implies that the person's job performance is less than what his test score indicates.)

Another way of expressing the research findings: Between-group differences in test performance are matched by corresponding group differences in job performance. (If minorities as a group score lower on the test, they also as a group tend to be less successful on the job.) Within each group, the lower test scoring person of either racial group also tends to be the poorer worker and the higher test scorer tends to be the more proficient worker. (If, for some reason, an employer decides to hire only minorities, a valid test would still be useful in identifying from among this group of applicants those with the highest probability of working out well on the job.)

Taken together, the research findings on this controversial topic would indicate that the same factors that lead to differences in test performance also lead to differences in job performance. This state of affairs holds for between-group as well as within-group differences. Stated another way, the evidence indicates that the same principles of behavior apply to minorities and nonminorities. Stripped of its emotional overtones, the conclusion makes sense: It makes sense that a job that requires a particular attribute, such as mechanical comprehension, for competent performance should require it of all incumbents and should require it to the same degree of minorities and nonminorities. In this context, accidents of birth are plainly irrelevant.

The answer cannot be concluded without these observations:

1. The findings reported above are based mostly on research studies that dealt with black-white comparisons. The few studies involving comparisons between whites and racial groups other than blacks have yielded results that are generally consistent with the picture for blacks and whites.

2. The research outcomes from the different studies are not uniformly in 1 direction; occasionally, "mixed" or "conflicting" findings are obtained. Overall, however, the evidence is decidedly in the direction of rejecting the differential validity hypothesis (this is the hypothesis that holds that tests have different meanings for different groups).

3. There are other models of test fairness besides the regression model associated with Cleary. Coverage of these other models is beyond the scope of this book. Suffice it to say that the Cleary regression model is the most widely accepted model of test fairness and it is consistent with the position of the federal government as expressed in the *Uniform Guidelines.*

4. Studies of test fairness involve relating test performance to job performance. The assumption is usually made that the measures of job performance employed are themselves unbiased.

By way of summary, bias in testing occurs when scores on the test do not accurately reflect the person's or group's abilities or skills. Scores on a typing test, for example, are said to be biased if the condition of the typewriter leads to inaccurate inferences about the typing ability of examinees. In the employment setting, tests are used as tools for determining who gets hired and who does not. The decision to hire Joe and not Jack is implicitly a prediction that Joe will be a better job performer than Jack. A test that is biased leads to inaccurate predictions of job performance in the sense that a job candidate's probability of successfully performing the job is not commensurate with the probability of his being selected for the job. Influences that are limited to test performance will lead to inaccurate predictions. Cultural factors that lower the test scores of minorities without also adversely affecting their job performance would bias the decision-making process in the direction that is unfair to minorities. As indicated above, the evidence suggests that employment tests are not biased against minorities.

Q-67 Who is more likely to fail the typical employment test— a minority or a nonminority job candidate?

Minorities as a group do less well on tests than their nonminority counterparts.

Q-68 How can employment tests not be biased when minorities tend to score lower than nonminorities?

Group differences in test performance, without more information, are not sufficient to establish that a test is biased or unfair. In order to make a judgment on a test's fairness, it is necessary to determine whether the lower scoring group on the test also scores low on the job. This requires a formal validation study of how different persons with different test scores perform on the job and of how the operational use of the test is likely to impact on the employment opportunities of persons from different groups. If the test identifies poor job performers and the test is used in such a way that "high test scorers-good job performers," whether they are minorities or nonminorities, are more likely to be selected for openings than "low test scorers-poor job performers," the test is not unfair. Stated differently, the notion of fairness has to do with whether a person's probability of doing well on the job is commensurate with his probability of being selected for the job. If it develops that proportionately more of the "low test scorers-poor job performers" come from the minority group and proportionately more of the "high test scorers-good job performers" come from the nonminority group, a fair test would show a higher passing rate for nonminorities. The test would have an adverse impact on minorities, but it would not be unfair to them.

Q-69 Does the previous answer imply that group differences in test performance are not significant?

No. Group differences in test performance are significant from at least the following points of view:

1. Adverse impact considerations. Group differences on the test will reveal themselves in such statistics as disparities in failure rates between minorities and nonminorities, disparities in passing rates, and disparities in selection rates—indices that are frequently used to gauge whether an employment practice has an adverse impact. The concept of adverse impact is a key concept in employment discrimination where the showing of adverse impact by the complaining party triggers the requirement on the part of the employer to show that the test is job related.

2. Affirmative action commitments. Organizations that do business with the U.S. government are required by Executive Order No. 11246 not only to refrain from unlawful discrimination but also to develop and implement affirmative action programs for the benefit of persons protected by Title VII of the Civil Rights Act of 1964, as amended. Where tests are used in the employment process, the generally observed differences in test performance between minorities and nonminorities complicate the job of meeting the human resources requirements of the business while simultaneously meeting the goals and timetables of an affirmative action program.

3. Determinants of group differences. There is an ongoing heated debate over the controversial and emotionally charged question of whether observed differences in test performance are due to genetic factors or to environmental factors.

The answer to the previous question was not intended to minimize the importance of the considerations listed above. Group differences in test performance are clearly relevant to the test's adverse impact, affect affirmative action commitments, and fuel the debate over the genesis of the observed group differences. Just because 1 group scores lower on a test than another group, however, does not necessarily mean that the test is biased or unfair. In addition to the statistics on differences on the test, one needs information on group differences on the criterion of job performance and of the relationship between test and job performance differences.

Q-70 Is it correct to say that test fairness is not a characteristic of the test?

Test fairness is not an inherent property of the test but of the manner in which a test is used operationally to make accept/reject decisions affecting job candidates from various cultural backgrounds. The consequences of test usage can be fair or unfair to some groups depending on whether members of the affected groups stand the same chance of being selected as they stand of doing the job successfully. If the same passing or qualification score on the test translates to the same level of performance on the job for both minorities and nonminorities, then use of the same cutoff score is fair and appropriate.

Q-71 Are group differences in test performance due to genetic or environmental factors?

The question is sometimes cast in terms of the so-called nature versus nurture dichotomy where it is understood that a child does not talk until it is old enough (nature effects) but the language it speaks is the language that it hears (nurture effects). Some preliminary comments:

1. The question, cast in general terms, is accepted as a research question and accorded the appropriate level of excitement (generally low). The same question, posed in the context of black-white differences in test performance, takes on a highly evaluative character and becomes the object of heated controversy. The reason for this differential reaction may have been eloquently captured by R. Flaugher (1978) when he noted the tendency to ascribe overinterpretations to group differences in test performance:

   A test of commonly encountered problems will not be called that but, rather, a test of "practical judgment." If the examinee is asked to offer suggestions, the word *creativity* will probably appear (in the test title). And a test of verbal, numerical and symbolic problems is far less likely to be called a "problems" test than a test of intelligence. The overinterpretation that occurs is not without its encouragement from the profession (of psychology). But when these tests are presented as assessments of highly valued parts of the spectrum, the issue of test bias is legitimately raised, since it is a great leap from being unable to work a few problems on a paper-and-pencil test to being declared lacking in "practical judgment." (p. 673)

2. It is also observed preliminarily that the evidence is fairly strong from studies reported in the professional literature dealing with black-white differences in test performance that the observed differences in favor of whites are not artifacts of the data nor of the sampling procedures but reflect populational differences between the 2 groups. That is to say, differences in mean test scores between the 2 groups are statistically significant. It should be added that even though the average test score of the white group is displaced upward relative to the average test score of the black group, there is substantial overlap between the 2 distributions. That is to say, the observed differences are group differences that do not preclude the finding that some blacks test out higher than some of their white counterparts.

3. When used in connection with the determinants of black-white differences in test performance, the term "environment" does not refer to an artificially created, abstract set of experimental conditions to which blacks are exposed for a brief period of time. Rather, the term encompasses a host of physical, psychological, and normative conditions—their implications and demand characteristics—that are frequently cumulative in their effects and often span a number of generations.

Against the foregoing background, this answer has the following elements: Environmental factors interact with biologic factors quite early in life to influence behavior. The 2 determinants of behavior become so inextricably intertwined that it becomes virtually impossible to tease out the contribution that is due to one's genes and those that are unique to one's circumstances. Some investigators have tried and have gained fame in the process. It is probably true that one's genetic endowment places an upper limit to what the human organism can achieve under the best of circumstances. Even in the best of circumstances, however, few people reach the limits of their potential. The gap between actual achievements and full potential widens as one's environment restricts access to the sorts of opportunities and influences that lead to culturally defined success. Group differences in test performance, however one may wish to allocate them between heredity and environment, do have practical implications. They imply that operational use of employment tests to arrive at selection decisions will most probably result in adverse impact and thereby trigger the requirement for validation. They also have implications for fulfilling the numerical objectives of an affirmative action program. For the personnel manager who properly views tests as managerial tools, the genesis of group differences is less important than their practical implications for the manner in which he ought to be planning for and addressing the human resources requirements of the business. Stated differently, the management of human resources can be adequately and responsibly discharged without knowing the precise blend of genetic and environmental factors that account for group differences in test performance. But the manager does need to know that these group differences exist, that he needs to structure his recruiting strategies in light of what is known about the magnitude of those differences vis-à-vis his employment standards, and that his records will most probably reflect adverse impact for the testing component of his employment process.

This discussion is intended to place observed group differences in test performance in some sort of perspective in addition to the strictly psychometric. For reasons that are elaborated upon in the concluding section of this book, the perspective chosen is managerial in tone—one that managers are likely to insist on, one that they can live with, and one that they can act upon. This view reflects no disillusionment with things psychometric; it merely suggests that it is time for management to "take it from here."

This is not to suggest that employment tests measure human attributes that are trivial or frivolous nor to suggest that the observed magnitude of group differences is some insignificant quantity. It is quite one thing, however, to develop a Freudian fixation on the origins of group differences and quite another to competently manage the reality and magnitude of those differences in the service of responsibly meeting the human resources needs of the workplace.

When understood against the perspective that is urged here, group differences in test performance become, like rising interest rates and Occupational Safety and Health Administration (OSHA) regulations, 1 more condition that must be factored into the complicated business of running the business. Unless it has been misjudged greatly, competent managers have the wherewithal to handle the adverse impact of tests in ways that would not adversely affect business operations or set back the goals of affirmative action programs.

Q-72   In a nutshell, what is the overall finding of studies investigating the question of differential validity?

The message is strong: The differential validity hypothesis that holds that tests may have different meanings for different groups is no longer professionally respectable.

Q-73   Would the same finding be obtained by researchers more sympathetic to the minority point of view?

The findings used to back up the conclusions in this book represent the outcome of studies utilizing professionally acceptable procedures that are equally applicable to and binding upon researchers without regard to their race, sex, age, religion, or national origin.

Q-74   What does the foregoing conclusion imply in practical terms?

The finding that tests behave the same way for minorities and nonminorities implies that if validity is shown for a test in a competently done validation study with white study subjects, the likelihood is high that the test will also be valid for other groups. Accordingly, the need diminishes to perform a separate validation study involving minority study subjects.

Q-75   Is this at variance with the Uniform Guidelines on Employee Selection Procedures?

The *Uniform Guidelines on Employee Selection Procedures* represent the administrative interpretation of equal employment opportunity law. While the *Uniform Guidelines* are intended to be consistent with the professional standards that psychologists develop in light of research results, occasional differences occur. In the area of differential validity, the *Uniform Guidelines* would require that fairness studies be conducted whenever technically feasible. This is equivalent to requiring that separate studies be conducted, whenever technically feasible, for minorities and nonminorities.

The applicable provision, Section 14B(8), reads as follows:

This section generally calls for studies of unfairness where technically feasible. The concept of fairness or unfairness of selection procedures is a developing concept. In addition, fairness studies generally require substantial numbers of employees in the job or group of jobs being studied. For these reasons, the Federal enforcement agencies recognize that the obligation to conduct studies of fairness imposed by the guidelines generally will be upon users or group of users with a large number of persons in a job class, or test developers; and that small users utilizing their own selection procedures will generally not be obligated to conduct such studies because it will be technically infeasible for them to do so.

This answer suggests that from a professional point of view, the need to conduct separate analyses for minorities in order to generate the necessary data for differential validity and fairness analyses is not as great as the need reflected in Section 14B(8) of the *Uniform Guidelines*. The consensus of professional opinion views the issue of differential validity as quite dead; the *Uniform Guidelines*, on the other hand, would require a showing that the issue is not alive and well.

Q-76   Is the discrepancy between professional standards and the Uniform Guidelines, exemplified in the previous discussion, an example of placing test users between a rock and a hard spot?

The answer recognizes the discrepancy between what the *Uniform Guidelines* would require and what the relevant research studies show and the reasonably compelling circumstance that test-using employers face with respect to complying with the *Uniform Guidelines*. Under the circumstances, the prudent practitioner would do well to perform the separate studies called for by Section 14B(8) whenever technically feasible.

Q-77 Is it possible to develop a test that favors minorities?

Yes, it is possible to build a test in which minority examinees would do better than their nonminority counterparts. R. Williams (1970), for example, devised a test consisting of items more familiar to blacks than to whites. Writing about the test, Williams notes:

At this time, the writer has developed a new approach to the study of ability by developing an intelligence test that is *biased* in favor of Black people. The name of the instrument is the "BITCH" test, which is translated "Black Intelligence Test Counterbalanced for Honkies." That is the adult form. I am also working on another test which is called "The S.O.B. Test," or the children's form. At first blush, you perhaps consider these tests as humorous. May I ask, "Is it more indicative of intelligence to know Malcom X's last name or the author of Hamlet?" I ask you now, "When is Washington's birthday?" Perhaps 99% of you thought February 22. That answer presupposes a white norm. I actually meant Booker T. Washington's birthday, not George Washington's. (p. 20)

Williams may have developed the BITCH test and its progeny, S.O.B., with tongue in cheek. Williams does illustrate that tests are instruments that are sensitive to and register the influence of one's environment. Tests do hear the language of the slums.

The discussion is rounded off with the following observations. First, cultural differences in test performance are more than statistical abstractions; they quickly and decisively turn into a handicap for those who must compete in a culture other than their own. Second, in industry and in other applied settings, tests are used as tools of prediction. Tests are useful to the extent that they enhance the accuracy of selection decisions by measuring legitimate job requirements—those characteristics that are related to job performance. The fact that members of some group may earn higher scores than members of other groups should not obscure the role of tests as instruments of prediction. Elsewhere the need to go beyond test scores has been addressed. The same care that goes into developing the test should be exerted at establishing the test's relevance to nontest outcomes, such as organizational criteria of job success. In other words, a validation study should be conducted to evaluate the significance of observed group differences in test performance, to determine if the same factors that depress or enhance test performance also depress or enhance job performance.

To conclude, this answer suggests that a person's behavior when taking a test or when performing his job is influenced by a host of cultural factors. Efforts directed only at looking at group differences in test performance without batting an eye in the direction of group differences in job performance represent half a loaf. A validation study goes a step further and ensures that the test is not a source of irrelevant difficulty. Beyond validation, the payoffs are greater when the problem is conceptualized as a problem not of remedying the effects of cultural factors on test performance but of utilizing tests to meet the human resources requirements of the business. The hypothesis here is that when employment testing is competently managed, it leads to the effective utilization of available talent without hurting an organization's affirmative action efforts.

Part III

EMPLOYMENT TESTING— THE LEGAL CONTEXT

Q-78 *Are employment tests prohibited by antidiscrimination laws?*

It is quite obvious that there are a number of laws enacted at various levels of government that ban discrimination with respect to the terms and conditions of employment. At the federal level, these antidiscrimination laws are typically supplemented by appropriate presidential executive orders, elaborated upon by means of regulations or guidelines issued by agencies such as the EEOC, and interpreted by court decisions. These laws and regulations are collectively referred to as "EEO laws" because they embody the fundamental notion of providing equal employment opportunity in the workplace. The observation that, in today's climate, every personnel decision represents a potential legal transaction, calls attention to the increasing number of EEO laws and to the breadth and scope of personnel activities that are covered by them.

No EEO law prohibits the use of employment tests as a personnel tool for meeting the human resources requirements of the enterprise. The so-called Tower Amendment, codified in Section 703(h) of Title VII of the Civil Rights Act of 1964, explicitly permits the use of employment tests in the following language:

nor shall it be an unlawful employment practice for an employer to give and to act upon the results of any professionally developed ability test provided such test, its administration or action upon the results, is not designed, intended, or used to discriminate because of race, color, religion, sex or national origin.

No interpretive guidelines or regulations from any of the federal agencies that administer the various EEO laws prohibit employment testing. The *Uniform Guidelines on Employee Selection Procedures,* the most detailed and highly developed set of guidelines governing the use of tests and other devices in arriving at employment decisions of various sorts, do not prohibit employment testing although some will argue that the *Uniform Guidelines* are so burdensome and difficult to comply with that they have the effect of discouraging employment testing.

To summarize, employment testing is not prohibited by any of the EEO laws or by any of the attendant guidelines issued by various agencies responsible for administering them. Developments since the passage of Title VII of the Civil Rights Act of 1964 have elaborated on the Tower Amendment by detailing the procedural and technical requirements that a user must satisfy in order to "give and to act upon the results of any professionally developed ability test." As rigorous and as stringent as these requirements are, they do not represent an outright ban against employment testing.

Q-79 What is the basic thrust of EEO laws?

The common element that runs across the various EEO laws is embodied in the basic principle that employment decisions should be based on a person's ability to do the job, not on accidents of birth such as age, race, sex, color, religion, or national origin. When tests are used to measure a person's ability to perform the job, accidents of birth have been found to result in lowered average test performance of minority examinees vis-à-vis their nonminority counterparts—a circumstance that triggers the requirement for a showing of job relatedness or test validity in order to overcome the test's adverse impact.

Q-80 Which EEO law has the most "teeth"?

There is no shortage of antidiscrimination prohibitions. B. Schlei and P. Grossman (1976) characterize the present state of affairs in this fashion:

Persons who believe themselves to be the victims of discrimination under Title VII will often have other avenues of redress in which they may assert the same or related claims. Thus, a claim of racial discrimination may be assertable under a contractual grievance procedure; a state fair employment practices act; the federal contract compliance program under Executive Order 11246, as amended; the Civil Rights Acts of 1866 and 1871; and a state's unemployment insurance program. The facts giving rise to a Title VII claim may also give rise to a claim which may be presented to the National Labor Relations Board as an alleged violation of the Taft-Hartley Act. A claim of sex discrimination under Title VII involving pay differences between men and women may also be cognizable under the Fair Labor Standards Act of 1938, as amended by the Equal Pay Act of 1963. (p. 943)

The quoted passage provides a glimpse of the multiplicity of EEO laws resulting in overlapping remedies against discrimination and of the various sources of protection for the aggrieved. Developments in the legal arena suggest that: An aggrieved individual may pursue his claims in different forums (for example, the federal court system or the grievance-arbitration machinery of collective bargaining); a person does not have to exhaust the remedies available under 1 forum before he can resort to another forum; and an unfavorable decision in 1 forum does not foreclose or invalidate parallel claims in another forum. The rationale for the foregoing scenario is articulated by the Supreme Court in its *Alexander v. Gardner-Denver Co.* decision (7FEP 81 (1974)):

In submitting his grievance to arbitration, an employee seeks to vindicate his contractual right under a collective bargaining agreement. By contrast, in filing a lawsuit under Title VII, an employee asserts independent statutory rights accorded by Congress. The distinctly separate nature of these contractual and statutory rights is not vitiated merely because both were violated as a result of the same factual occurrence.

Given the multiple avenues of relief and the interrelationships among the various sources of protection, it is not surprising that the legal profession finds itself playing an increasingly visible role in historically personnel functions—drawn into the action by exigencies that range from an employer's desire to understand the underlying questions of law to advice on minimizing the adverse publicity arising from an unfavorable court decision.

Title VII is not without "teeth," with remedies ranging from discontinuance of the discriminatory practice to monetary relief for the victims of discrimination (see *Q–83*). Title VII is also quite well developed: Even though other sources of protection are available, they are frequently invoked in tandem with Title VII or, where they are invoked alone, their application has been patterned after Title VII. Some of the landmark cases in the area of employment testing also have been decided under Title VII. Hence, in order to keep this part of the book from escalating into a legal treatise, attention will focus on developments surrounding Title VII of the Civil Rights Act of 1964.

Q-81   Who enforces Title VII?

Title VII is enforced by means of legal actions brought either by agencies of the federal government or by private individuals. Under the 1972 amendments of Title VII of the Civil Rights Act of 1964, the EEOC was empowered to bring suits involving so-called pattern and practice of discrimination. Prior to the 1972 amendments, these "pattern and practice" lawsuits were reserved for the Attorney General. The 1972 amendments also empowered the EEOC to institute civil proceedings in private actions after its conciliation efforts have failed.

The more common vehicle for enforcing Title VII is through individual plaintiffs acting as private attorneys general to vindicate a national policy that was accorded high priority by Congress. And when the individual plaintiff is successful in the courts, he not only wins for himself as a private citizen but also advances the public objective of dismantling discriminatory employment practices.

Q-82   How is Title VII enforced?

The procedural mechanism for resolving discrimination complaints under Title VII involves 2 distinct processes: the administrative (concilation) and the judicial (court proceedings).

The administrative machinery is designed to resolve charges of discrimination informally through conciliation and involves the agency created by Title VII—the EEOC as well as state and local agencies with jurisdiction over the charge. The idea behind conciliation is to achieve Title VII's objective of eradicating discrimination by means of voluntary settlements, short of expensive and time-consuming litigation. In order to give the administrative machinery maximum opportunity to work, Congress mandated that all charges of discrimination must first be filed with the EEOC before reaching the courthouse and accorded conciliation discussions a high degree of confidentiality. Thus, no one may bypass the EEOC on his way to the courtroom; when filed with the EEOC, the charge of discrimination triggers the administrative machinery for voluntarily settling charges deemed to be meritorious.

The judicial mechanism for enforcing Title VII starts with the filing of a lawsuit in the appropriate federal District Court and goes through the processes and activities associated with litigation (for example, discovery, trial, appeals). Compared with the administrative conciliation process, litigation is more complex, more expensive, and more time consuming.

Q-83   What are the penalties for violations of Title VII?

Upon a finding of illegal discrimination, the trial judge in a Title VII case is vested with broad remedial powers that include:

a. injunctions prohibiting continued use of the discriminatory employment practice (tests or educational requirements, for example, may be discontinued if they are found to be not job related);

b. relief for identifiable victims of discrimination in the form of reinstatement of discharged employees, adjustment of seniority rosters, and admission to union membership (the notion here is to restore identifiable victims of discrimination to their rightful place—where they would have been but for the illegal discriminatory behavior);

c. imposition of numerical quotas designed to correct severe statistical disparities in the composition of defendant employer's workforce brought about by past illegal discrimination;

d. monetary relief in the form of back pay awards designed to "make whole" the victims of unlawful discrimination; and

e. assessment of attorneys' fees.

The arsenal of remedies available to courts to correct the effects of discrimination can be characterized as broad in scope, intended to give the District Court judge the discretion to fashion the most complete relief possible. The authority for the exercise of Title VII remedies is grounded in the Act itself:

If the court finds that the respondent has intentionally engaged in or is intentionally engaging in an unlawful employment practice charged in the complaint, the court may enjoin the respondent from engaging in such unlawful employment practice, and order such affirmative action as may be appropriate, which may include but is not limited to, reinstatement or hiring of employees, with or without backpay (payable by the employer, employment agency or labor organization, as the case may be, responsible for the unlawful employment practice), or any other equitable relief as the court deems appropriate. (Sec. 706(g))

Q-84 In view of the backlog of cases at the EEOC, why shouldn't an aggrieved person go straight to the courthouse?

The practice of filing a charge with the EEOC prior to instituting court action represents congressional preference for resolving claims of discrimination through administrative channels rather than through protracted litigation. Over time, the effect of many such voluntary settlements is to achieve Title VII's objective of eliminating unlawful employment practices without the costs of litigation. The buildup of cases awaiting to be processed is a natural consequence of allowing the administrative machinery of the EEOC the opportunity to work.

The suggestion to bypass the EEOC's conciliation process for the purpose of alleviating the current backlog of charges would frustrate congressional intent and is tantamount to suggesting that we suspend trial of criminal cases because our jails are overcrowded.

Q-85   What are the ground rules for a Title VII lawsuit?

Title VII lawsuits are civil actions and are commenced in the appropriate federal District Court by the timely filing of a complaint. Two major concepts underlie the prosecution of a Title VII lawsuit: jurisdictional prerequisities and the order and allocation of burden of proof. Each is discussed in turn.

Before a lawsuit can begin its progress through the legal process, the complaining party must satisfy 2 preliminary requirements and do so within established time frames. First, he must file a charge of discrimination with the EEOC within 180 days of the occurrence of the alleged discriminatory practice. In so-called deferral states that have agencies with jurisdiction over the charge, the filing period with the EEOC is extended to within 300 days of the occurrence of the complained of practice or within 30 days of receiving notice that local or state proceedings have been terminated, whichever is earlier. The second prerequisite pertains to the timely filing of the lawsuit—something that must be accomplished within 90 days after receipt of a notice of right to sue from the EEOC. The requirements for the timely filing of a charge with the EEOC and the timely filing of a lawsuit are considered jurisdictional prerequisities in the sense that failure to comply with them represents sufficient grounds for dismissing the complaint.

The order and allocation of burden of proof refers to the sequence and type of evidence that either side to the dispute needs in order to sustain their case. The plaintiff has the initial burden of establishing a prima facie face of discrimination by showing, for example, that he was treated more harshly than nonprotected group members (disparate treatment) or that he was subjected to a seemingly neutral procedure with an adverse impact on classes protected by Title VII (disparate impact). If the plaintiff is successful in carrying out this initial burden, the ball goes to the defendant's court. The defendant must show that the complained of practice is legitimate and justified by business necessity. When an employment test is involved, the defendant must be prepared to show that the test is job related (usually by means of a validation study) and therefore legitimate despite its adverse impact. The burden subsequently shifts back to the plaintiff to rebut the defendant's claim by showing, in the case of employment testing, that other procedures are available to the defendant with substantially equal validity but lesser adverse impact.

The foregoing is a condensed version of the general procedural framework for Title VII actions. Much of the early litigation activity was directed at the more mechanical aspects for bringing suit. The timeliness requirements for filing a charge with the EEOC and for filing of a lawsuit were extended to their present limits when the Civil Rights Act was amended in 1972. Hence, the present ground rules reflect both litigation and congressional activity.

Q-86 What is a class action lawsuit?

A class action lawsuit is one brought by an aggrieved person on his behalf and on behalf of all others who are similarly situated. Rule 23 of the Federal Rules of Civil Procedure specifies the conditions that must be satisfied in order to maintain the suit as a class action. The conditions generally pertain to the ability of the named plaintiff(s) to represent adequately the interests of the class and to the propriety of using the class as an efficient mechanism for resolving multiple controversies involving substantially the same facts, issues, and defenses.

Class actions are predictably more complicated and more dangerous for the employer than individual actions. Depending on the size of the class, the employer's potential back pay liability could run conservatively into 6-digit figures. Notice to members of the class may be required in order to announce such developments as the terms of an out-of-court settlement or their entitlement to court-imposed remedies secured by the named plaintiffs.

Q-87 Are EEO laws here to stay?

The author's sentiments are fairly summarized in the following observation made almost 15 years ago by a publication of the American Petroleum Institute:

The Civil Rights Act of 1964 is now the law of the land. Its enforcement is still far from complete, but it is unlikely that the act will be repealed or that the machinery for its enforcement will be weakened. (*Equal Employment Opportunity: An Interpretive Guide*, p. 53)

Q-88 What testing cases have been decided by the Supreme Court?

The Supreme Court does not hear every appeal that it receives. It is estimated that only 10% of the cases sent to the Supreme Court are heard by the highest legal authority in the land. Accordingly, those cases that are heard by the Supreme Court tend to be granted landmark status. Two of the Title VII cases in the testing area are discussed below.

Griggs v. Duke Power Company (3 FEP 175 (1971)) was the first testing case to be heard by the Supreme Court; it was decided in 1971. The lower courts had earlier recognized that the tests in question that were not validated disqualified more blacks than whites but saw no violation of Title VII since the requirements were applied to blacks and whites alike. The Supreme Court disagreed, holding that "the Act proscribes not only overt discrimination, but also practices that are fair in form, but discriminatory in operation." Accordingly, the Supreme Court continued, "practices, procedures or tests which are neutral on their face, and even neutral in terms of intent" but that have an adverse impact, are in violation of Title VII unless it can be shown, and it is the employer's burden to show, that "they have a manifest relationship to the employment in question."

The significance of the *Griggs* decision derives from its explicit recognition of the disparate impact theory of discrimination. It will be recalled that the lower courts saw no violation of Title VII based on the disparate treatment point of view. For most personnel practices that are standardized to ensure uniformity of administration, scoring, and interpretation, the disparate treatment theory is less of a problem than the uneven consequences flowing from their application. Clearly, a manager can control the incidence of disparate treatment allegations by insisting that standard procedures are adhered to. Adverse impact is more difficult to control (see discussion in *Q-94*).

The second testing case was decided by the Supreme Court in 1975 in the case of *Albemarle Paper Co. et al. v. Moody et al.* (10 FEP 1181 (1975)). The tests at issue in the *Albemarle* case were validated using the concurrent study in which present employees are used as subjects in the validation effort. Details of the validation study, recounted in the Supreme Court's opinion, leave the most fervent test-loving person convinced that no validation study is better than a poorly conducted study. The Supreme Court, citing provisions from the EEOC's 1970 guidelines on employment testing procedures as a yardstick for evaluating the adequacy of *Albemarle*'s validity evidence, enumerated major deficiencies in the validation study to support the Court's conclusion that the study was materially flawed and defective in several important respects. Many industrial psychologists may disagree with the Supreme Court's use of the EEOC guidelines for measuring the adequacy of validation studies but few of them will disagree that *Albemarle*'s validation effort fell short of commonly accepted professional standards.

The lesson from *Albemarle* seems to be that the long arm of the law touches those studies first that are technically deficient. Between them, *Griggs* and *Albemarle* laid the cornerstone for the fundamentals of employment testing litigation under Title VII. The major elements are captured in 2 propositions:

A. Employment tests that have an adverse impact on classes protected by Title VII, even though neutral on their face and neutral in intent, must be shown to be job related to survive challenge.

B. Job relatedness of employee selection procedures is shown by competent validity evidence obtained from a study conducted along the lines spelled out in governmental guidelines on testing.

Q-89   What is adverse impact?

Adverse impact refers to substantial disparities in the rate with which different groups are affected by personnel decisions involving their employment opportunities. This definition is sufficiently generic to accommodate various kinds of personnel decisions (such as selection, promotion, transfer, termination) and sufficiently broad to allow for the possibility that personnel decisions could operate to the disadvantage of majority as well as minority group members. Where an employment test is concerned, adverse impact may take on the form of significant differences in qualification or "passing" rates between minority and nonminority examinees.

Adverse impact is a way of gauging, in quantitative terms, the consequences of personnel decisions on different groups. The term is an EEO buzz word that is most frequently associated with minorities who have historically been more harshly affected by personnel decisions of various sorts.

Q-90   Why is the concept of adverse impact important?

For two major reasons. First, adverse impact recognizes that form of discrimination that occurs when, in the language of the Supreme Court in *Griggs, v. Duke Power Co.* (3 FEP 175(1971)), "practices, procedures, or tests which are neutral on their face, and even neutral in terms of intent, may be discriminatory in operation" because their operational use affects some groups more harshly than others. An employment test, for example, even though it is required of all applicants and is administered in a standardized, uniform fashion becomes suspect when it works to the disadvantage of minorities whose passing rate on the test is substantially lower than that of nonminorities. In other words, treating all individuals the same way by subjecting them, for example, to the same testing process does not guarantee that the consequences will be the same for all groups.

The second major reason for the importance of the concept of adverse impact lies in its role in the enforcement scheme of various EEO laws and regulations. Under Title VII, employment practices that have an adverse impact on protected groups are presumed to be discriminatory unless they are justified by business necessity or demonstrated to be job related. Under Executive Order 11246 and the attendant Revised Order No. 4 issued by the Office of Contract Compliance Programs, adverse impact is expressed in terms of the underutilization of women and minorities in specific job classifications relative to the applicable labor market. Where underutilization reaches proportions that render the federal contractor in noncompliance with the affirmative action provisions of Revised Order No. 4, the employer becomes subject to the sanctions of cancellation, termination, or suspension of existing government contracts and debarment from future contracts. Adverse impact is thus the trigger that sets in motion the various mechanisms associated with the enforcement of EEO laws.

Q-91 How is adverse impact measured?

The generic formula calls for computing the percentage of protected group members affected by the employment practice in question and comparing that figure with the corresponding figure for the nonprotected group. For example, suppose that 20 females are hired out of 50 applicants, while 30 males are hired out of 50 applicants. The resulting selection rates would be .40 for females and .60 for males. Suppose further that both groups of applicants were subjected to the same set of employment tests where 40 of the 50 female applicants passed, while 45 of the 50 male applicants passed. The resulting test passing rates are .80 for females and .90 for males. The table below summarizes the outcome of these computations:

Applicants	Test Passing Rate		Selection Rate	
50 females	(40/50)	.80	(20/50)	.40
50 males	(45/50)	.90	(30/50)	.60

The next step after the computations is to evaluate the magnitude of the observed differences (if any) between the groups. Is the selection or passing rate for 1 group substantially less than the corresponding rate for the other group? The *Uniform Guidelines* adopt the so-called 4/5ths or 80% rule of thumb for assessing the significance of the disparities in selection rates. According to the 4/5ths rule, adverse impact is normally indicated when 1 selection rate is less that 80% of the other. When the 4/5ths rule is applied to the simplified example, it is seen that adverse impact is indicated for the selection rate since the female rate of .40 is less that .48 (which is 80% of the .60 rate for males) but no adverse impact is indicated for the test passing rate where the 2 groups are within approximately 90% of each other's passing rates.

Q-92 Is the 4/5ths rule an official way of determining adverse impact?

The 4/5ths rule is in the nature of a rule of thumb, adopted by the drafters of the *Uniform Guidelines* to provide test users with a practical guide for assessing the existence of adverse impact. The *Uniform Guidelines* and the set of questions and answers issued on March 2, 1979 to clarify and interpret the *Uniform Guidelines* (See Federal Register, vol. 44, no. 43, 1979) make the following points about the 4/5ths rule:

1. The 4/5ths rule does not constitute a legal definition of discrimination.

The Guidelines adopt a "rule of thumb" as a practical means of determining adverse impact for use in enforcement proceedings. The rule is known as the "4/5ths" or "80 percent" rule. It is not a legal definition of discrimination, rather it is a practical device to keep the attention of enforcement agencies on serious discrepancies in hire or promotion rates or other employment decisions. (*Uniform Guidelines*, Section II)

2. The 4/5ths rule is not a license that permits 20% discrimination.

The 4/5ths rule of thumb speaks only to the question of adverse impact, and is not intended to resolve the ultimate question of unlawful discrimination. Regardless of the amount of differences in selection rates, unlawful discrimination may be present, and may be demonstrated through appropriate evidence. The 4/5ths rule merely establishes a numerical basis for drawing an initial inference and for requiring additional information. [Answer to Question 19.]

3. The 4/5ths rule is not the only way of determining the existence of adverse impact.

Where large numbers of selections are made, relatively small differences in selection rates may nevertheless constitute adverse impact if they are both statistically and practically significant. For that reason, if there is a small difference in selection rates (one rate is more than 80% of the other) but large numbers of selections are involved, it would be appropriate to calculate the statistical significance of the difference in selection rates. [Answer to Question 22.]

4. The 4/5ths rule is applied first to "bottom line" statistics and, as indicated, to components of the overall selection process.

Adverse impact is determined first for the overall selection process for each job. If the overall selection process has an adverse impact, the adverse impact of the individual selection procedure should be analyzed. For any selection procedure in the process having an adverse impact which the user continued to use in the same manner, the user is expected to have evidence of validity satisfying the Guidelines. [Answer to Question 13.]

Q-93 What is meant by the bottom-line concept of adverse impact?

The bottom-line concept refers to the selection rates that result from the operation of the overall selection process (whose components, for example, may include testing, the interview, and reference checks). If there is no adverse impact on the basis of overall bottom-line statistics, the *Uniform Guidelines* provide that the individual components need not be evaluated for adverse impact or validated.

Adoption of the bottom-line concept by the drafters of the *Uniform Guidelines* provides an easy-to-use mechanism for directing the resources of the enforcing agencies to those users whose overall selection processes have an adverse impact. Of 2 users, the 1 with adverse impact based on bottom-line statistics is seen as the more fruitful target of "administrative and prosecutorial discretion.'' The bottom-line concept is thus a management tool for allocating enforcement resources rather than a legally controlling parameter of discrimination.

The bottom-line concept resembles the compensatory philosophy embodied in the multiple regression strategy of combining pre-employment data (see *Q-13*). In the multiple regression model, an applicant with low scores on 1 component of the overall selection process (who would otherwise be disqualified from further consideration by virtue of this low performance) may end up qualified for the job if he does very well on other components of the selection process. Since it is the person's overall performance that determines his job suitability, the person with a low score on one component may end up with a total aggregate score that puts him in the ''qualified'' category. It was noted in the discussion in *Q-13* that it is the person with a ''hills and valleys'' profile of pre-employment data who is most likely to profit from a compensatory strategy. In much the same way, the employer with unfavorable adverse impact statistics on each component of the overall selection process is not likely to benefit from the bottom-line concept.

Elsewhere (see *Q-19*), the view was expressed that a global approach to assessing applicant qualifications is a sensible business practice, particularly in those instances where the applicant just missed the cutoff score on the test. In these borderline situations, the applicant's nontest credentials may be sufficiently strong to affect the applicant's overall qualifications. If the person ends up being selected for the job, his failure to meet test standards would contribute to the adverse impact of the testing component but his selection would positively affect bottom-line results. It can be seen that, over many such decisions, the bottom-line approach to determining the existence of adverse impact gives credit for the judicious use of judgment in so-called borderline cases.

Q-94 Besides the 4/5ths rule and the bottom-line concept, what does an employment manager have to be concerned about with respect to adverse impact?

Two major items need to be added to the list. First, because adverse impact is a quantitative concept, statistics will play an increasingly important and pervasive role in the administration and enforcement of EEO laws. Statistics is a fairly straightforward discipline that deals with organizing data or with making inferences about certain populational characteristics based on limited sample data. Complications arise when experts are unable to agree on what sorts of data ought to be collected or when the outcome of statistical analysis yields results that are open to differing interpretations. When these complications develop, the stage is set for a battle of experts. One trial judge who presided over an employment discrimination lawsuit described his experience of being led through a labyrinth of statistical analysis as one that might well have intimidated Odysseus.

The second item that Odysseus and the employment manager should recognize is that adverse impact is not an unambiguous concept. W. R. Manese (1979) has summarized the major ambiguities in 3 general categories:

A. *Metric problems.* How should adverse impact be measured—by evaluating differences in passing rates, in failure rates, or in overall qualification rates? Should the selection rate be computed on the basis of all the applicants or should the computation be based on those examinees who qualified on the test or on those who have survived a particular hurdle in the selection process?

B. *Quantum problems.* How much adverse impact is sufficient to make out a presumptive case of unlawful discrimination? What if the 4/5ths rule and conventional tests of statistical significance yield conflicting answers?

C. *Standard-of-comparison problems.* With what reference population should discrepancies in selection rates be compared? Some of the possibilities include the so-called Standard Metropolitan Statistical Area (SMSA), the local labor market, the undifferentiated applicant population, or the employer's applicant pool.

The ambiguities associated with the concept of adverse impact stem in large measure from the fact that a given employment practice is embedded in widely differing personnel contexts and organizational exigencies. Hence, the answers to some of the issues posed above are dependent on an employer's particular set of circumstances at any given point in time. It is not surprising then that the relevant issues may not be reached with a high degree of specificity until a discrimination lawsuit forces both parties in the dispute to put a fence around the particular parameters of the case. The point of this discussion is not to titillate the imagination but to illustrate the ambiguities that surround a key concept in employment discrimination— adverse impact.

Q-95 Will running more applicants through the selection process lessen its adverse impact?

No. Running more applicants through the selection process will not affect the adverse impact picture either on a bottom-line basis or any component of the overall selection process. The testing component, for example, will disqualify minorities and nonminorities at the same comparative rates whether 100 or 1,000 examinees are run through it. Increasing the intake at the front end will not affect disparities in qualification rates unless recruiting efforts are differentially directed to increase the calibre of some applicant groups and not others.

Q-96 What is the relationship between the bottom-line concept and group differences in test performance?

Studies of group differences in test performance have generally found minority examinees scoring lower on paper-and-pencil employment tests than their nonminority counterparts and females scoring lower than males on physical ability measures. Thus, if adverse impact exists on a bottom-line basis, the odds are high that adverse impact would be found for the testing component of the selection process, thereby triggering the need to show validation evidence for the test(s) or measures in question.

Q-97 How is disparate treatment different from disparate or adverse impact?

Disparate treatment, also called intentional or overt discrimination, occurs when persons are treated differently because of their protected class status. Disparate or unequal treatment is the form of discrimination that is not difficult to recognize; it is also the form of discrimination that most people are familiar with. The elements of a disparate treatment theory of discrimination in a Title VII context were spelled out by the Supreme Court in the following language:

The complainant in a Title VII trial must carry the initial burden under the statute of establishing a prima facie case of racial discrimination. This may be done by showing (i) that he belongs to a racial minority; (ii) that he applied and was qualified for a job for which the employer was seeking applicants; (iii) that, despite his qualifications, he was rejected and (iv) that, after his rejection, the position remained open and the employer continued to seek applicants from persons of complainant's qualifications. (*McDonnell Douglas Corp. v. Green,* 5 FEP 965 (1973)).

While disparate treatment is associated with the overt, uneven treatment based on classifications (for example, race, sex, or national origin) forbidden by Title VII, adverse impact refers to the uneven consequences that result from the uniform application of some facially neutral procedure or practice. An employment test that is required of all job candidates to whom it is administered in a uniform way and that has the same passing score for minorities and nonminorities would not be considered discriminatory from the disparate treatment point of view but it would be suspect from the disparate or adverse impact point of view if the passing rates are substantially different for minority and nonminority examinees. The adverse impact theory of discrimination is particularly applicable to those practices that are neutral on their face but whose effects operate to the disadvantage of protected groups. Adverse impact is most frequently the basis for charges that employment tests of various sorts are discriminatory.

Q-98   Is the EEOC antitesting?

The Equal Employment Opportunity Commission was created to administer Title VII of the Civil Rights Act of 1964. In carrying out its role, the EEOC has engaged in the generic activities described below. None of these activities is designed to endear the EEOC to management or to test-loving peoples.

1. The EEOC participates in particularly significant litigation by filing *amicus curiae* (friend of the court) briefs on behalf of plaintiffs claiming to be victims of discriminatory practices. The early employment discrimination cases went against defendant employers, creating an early association between the EEOC and the agony of defeat.

2. The EEOC is a party to a number of consent decrees that have resulted in the utilization of women and minorities at a rate more accelerated than contemplated by the companies involved. Invariably, complying with the terms of the decree involves elaborate record-keeping requirements and detailed reporting procedures for monitoring the company's progress.

3. The EEOC is an integral part of the administrative machinery for processing a discrimination complaint. In the course of investigating a charge of discrimination, the Act allows EEOC to have access to records and information relevant to the employment practice(s) under challenge. In instances where probable cause exists to believe that the charges of discrimination have merit, the EEOC proceeds to rectify the situation by informal methods of conference, conciliation, and persuasion.

4. The EEOC is identified with the *Uniform Guidelines on Employee Selection Procedures,* a document that is "designed to assist employers, labor organizations, employment agencies, and licensing certification boards to comply with requirements of Federal law" (Sec. 1(B)). Some of the provisions (for example, those dealing with suitable alternatives or studies of test fairness) are seen as being unduly burdensome while others (for example, methods of test use) are regarded as uninvited intrusions into the affairs of the test user.

5. The 1972 amendments to Title VII gave the EEOC the authority to bring enforcement actions in the courts. Prior to 1972, the EEOC dealt with alleged unlawful employment practices by the informal methods of conference, conciliation, and persuasion. As the EEOC exercises the latest addition to its arsenal of enforcement powers, the relationship between the agency and the targets of its enforcement activities is not likely to improve.

Few governmental agencies have changed the landscape of the personnel manager's turf more than the EEOC. In the testing area, the EEOC has issued a series of guidelines for proper test development and test use. As each successive version has become more explicit in what a test user must do in order to comply, the burden of compliance has increased. It is not difficult to see why the EEOC could be perceived as being antitesting.

Q-99   *What are the major items in the* Uniform Guidelines on Employee Selection Procedures?

The *Uniform Guidelines on Employee Selection Procedures* were adopted on August 25, 1978 by the EEOC, the Civil Service Commission, and the Departments of Justice and Labor. At the time the *Uniform Guidelines* were published, two sets of federal testing guidelines were in existence: the so-called Federal Executive Agency (FEA) guidelines adopted by the Civil Service Commission and the Departments of Justice and Labor and the 1970 EEOC guidelines. The *Uniform Guidelines* superseded both as of September 25, 1978.

Those who have followed the evolution of governmental testing guidelines through their many iterations are able to discern differences between different versions at an exhausting level of microscopic detail. The interest, however, is on the major items presented below.

1. The adoption of a single set of guidelines is significant considering that prior efforts by the same issuing agencies to develop a uniform federal position resulted in the Scylla and Charybdis of the FEA and EEOC guidelines. The *Uniform Guidelines* are not likely to make a test user's burden of demonstrating the job relatedness of his employee selection procedures any lighter; they will, however, lead to the use of a single standard for assessing the adequacy of validation studies.

2. The precursor (FEA and EEOC) guidelines defined "test" in broad, expansive terms that effectively covered virtually every procedure on the basis of which employment decisions of various sorts are made. The *Uniform Guidelines* show no change in the scope of what is covered:

   These guidelines apply to tests and other selection procedures which are used as a basis for any employment decision. Employment decisions include, but are not limited to hiring, promotion, demotion, membership (for example, in a labor organization), referral, retention, and licensing and certification, to the extent that licensing and certification may be covered by Federal equal employment opportunity law. Other selection decisions, such as selection for training or transfer, may also be considered employment decisions if they lead to any of the decisions listed above. (Sec. 2(B))

3. The *Uniform Guidelines* adopt the bottom-line concept of adverse impact that provides that if the overall selection process (whose components, for example, may include testing, the interview, and a medical evaluation) results in no adverse impact, the individual components do not have to be evaluated for adverse impact or validated (see *Q-93*). In a situation where tests are used to screen applicants for employment, comparative hiring (bottom line) rates are examined for evidence of adverse impact before looking at comparative passing (component) rates on the test.

4. The reduction of the adverse impact of selection procedures is a recurring theme in the *Uniform Guidelines*. Section 3B, for example, requires test users to consider alternative selection procedures that are substantially equally valid and

to use the procedure with the lesser adverse impact. Some have argued that the search for suitable alternatives could develop into a never-ending task, somewhat like a cosmic search for the negative. Precisely what is intended by the *Uniform Guidelines* and the limits to the searching behavior are not clear from the language of Section 3B. It is clear, however, from the background section that precedes the technical portion of the *Uniform Guidelines* that test users are required to make the attempt:

Federal equal employment opportunity law has added a requirement to the process of validation. In conducting a validation study, the employer should consider available alternatives which will achieve its legitimate purpose with lesser adverse impact. (Part IV of Supplementary Information)

The same concern for minimizing adverse impact is evident in the provision dealing with how validated tests are used. Tests may be used to make selection decisions in 1 of several progressively stringent ways, including as a screening device (pass/fail), as a method for sorting examinee applicants into broad categories (for example, not qualified, intermediate, qualified) based on test score ranges, and as a device for ranking applicants based on their raw test scores with selections made from the top of the list. The *Uniform Guidelines* require test users to justify (for example, with a higher degree of validity) test usages that result in greater adverse impact. Thus, the last usage involving ranking would presumably require a higher level of validity than pass/fail test usage.

5. The *Uniform Guidelines* recognize the parity between content, construct, and criterion-related validation strategies for demonstrating job relatedness. This position is consistent with professional standards and represents a change from the 1970 EEOC guidelines, which showed a marked preference for criterion-related studies. The Supreme Court, in a footnote to its *Washington v. Davis* decision, expressed the same point of view, indicating that each strategy was equally appropriate in the right circumstances.

6. The *Uniform Guidelines* call for investigations of test fairness in order to determine whether selection procedures work the same way for all groups. Procedurally, the provision requires that validation data be collected separately for different race/sex groups in order to perform the necessary comparative statistical analyses. The obligation to conduct test fairness studies falls heavier on larger test users:

The Federal enforcement agencies recognize that the obligation to conduct studies of fairness imposed by the Guidelines generally will be upon users or groups of users with a large number of persons in a job class, or test developers; and that small users utilizing their own selection procedures will generally not be obligated to conduct such studies because it will be technically infeasible for them to do so. (Sec. 14B(8))

7. Some of the noteworthy items that remained substantially unchanged from either the FEA or the 1970 EEOC guidelines include the following:

   A. *Selection for higher than entry-level jobs.* The *Uniform Guidelines* retain the so-called flow-through provision, which gives test users the flexibility of gearing their selection procedures for higher than entry-level positions if it can be shown that the attainment of these higher level jobs is realistic:

If job progression structures are so established that employees will probably, within a reasonable period of time and in a majority of cases, progress to a higher level, it may be considered that the applicants are being evaluated for a job or jobs at the higher level. (Sec. 5(I))

B. *Interim use of selection procedures.* Under certain circumstances, a user may act on the results of a selection procedure in making operational selection decisions without waiting for the validation study to be completed:

Users may continue the use of a selection procedure which is not at the moment fully supported by the required evidence of validity, provided: (1) the user has available substantial evidence of validity and (2) the user has in progress, when technically feasible, a study which is designed to produce the additional evidence required by these guidelines within a reasonable time. (Sec. 5(J))

The provision is not without strings, however:

If the study does not demonstrate validity, this provision of these guidelines for interim use shall not constitute a defense in any action, nor shall it relieve the user of any obligations arising under Federal law. (Sec. 5 (J))

C. *Retesting.* The *Uniform Guidelines* recognize the need to offer unsuccessful examinees the chance to be retested consistent with the test user's need to safeguard the continued security of his selection procedures.

Users should provide a reasonable opportunity for retesting and reconsideration. Where examinations are administered periodically with public notice, such reasonable opportunity exists, unless persons who have previously been tested are precluded from retesting. The user may, however, take reasonable steps to preserve the security of its procedures. (Sec. 12)

D. *Casual assumption of validity.* The *Uniform Guidelines* insist on rigorous methodologies (for example, content, construct, or criterion-related validation studies) for demonstrating the job relatedness of selection procedures and continue the earlier rejection of testimonials as a substitute for evidence of validity:

Under no circumstances will the general reputation of a test or other selection procedures, its author or its publisher, or casual reports of its validity be accepted in lieu of evidence of validity. Specifically ruled out are: assumptions of validity based on a procedure's name or descriptive labels; all forms of promotional literature; data bearing on the frequency of a procedure's usage; testimonial statements and credentials of sellers, users or consultants; and other nonempirical or anecdotal accounts of selection practices or selection outcomes. (Sec. 9(A))

E. *Technical standards.* The technical standards for validity studies embodied in Section 14 of the *Uniform Guidelines* are generally consistent with their earlier counterparts but are much more detailed.

Q–100 How are the Uniform Guidelines *different from professional standards on test validation and test use?*

Some introductory comments about professional standards. The first set of professional standards was published by the American Psychological Association (APA) in 1966. Titled *Standards for Educational and*

Psychological Tests and Manuals, the document was geared primarily toward test developers and test producers. In 1974, the APA *Standards* were revised in the direction that recognized the needs of the test user whose practices had come under increasing public and legal scrutiny during the intervening years. In 1975, Division 14 of the APA, the Division or Specialty Field of Industrial and Organizational Psychology, published *Principles for the Validation and Use of Personnel Selection Procedures.* The Division 14 *Principles* sought to clarify the applicability of the APA *Standards* to the validation, use, and implementation of tests in the workplace. The Division 14 *Principles* were revised in 1980.

The foregoing account indicates that presently there are 2 sources of professional guidance in the area of test development and test validation: The APA *Standards* and the Division 14 *Principles.* For the purpose of the present discussion, they are referred to collectively as the professional standards. The *Uniform Guidelines* of the federal government are intended to be "consistent with generally accepted professional standards for evaluating standardized tests and other selection procedures" (Sec. 5(C)) such as those outlined in the APA *Standards.* There are differences. Rather than go through a blow-by-blow account of how the professional standards and the *Uniform Guidelines* address specific issues, we see the major divergencies between them as arising principally from the following sources:

1. The *Uniform Guidelines on Employee Selection Procedures* are a blend of technical standards, administrative policies, and interpretive statements of equal employment opportunity law. The *Uniform Guidelines* have a checklist characteristic, rendering them particularly suitable as an enforcement tool for assessing whether the test user is in compliance with specific provisions. The professional standards, on the other hand, are more collegial in tone and specify standards of good practice in terms that leave room for the exercise of professional discretion. The difference in orientation between the professional standards and the *Uniform Guidelines* is exemplified by the level of detail with which the outcome of validation studies is reported. Validation studies are reported in professional journals or in technical reports with only as much documentation as will permit another researcher to independently replicate the study or to evaluate the soundness of the procedures that the original investigator employed and the extent to which the conclusions drawn are justified by the data. On the other hand, the documentation requirements of the *Uniform Guidelines* are written to enable the field investigator to make the series of yes-no decisions that determine whether probable cause exists to believe that a validation study is deficient.

2. The professional standards articulate ideals that a practitioner should strive to achieve. The adequacy of a validation study is not dependent on literally satisfying each stated standard or principle. The *Uniform Guidelines,* in contrast, are stated as minimum standards: "The following minimum standards, as applicable, should be met in conducting a validity study" (Sec. 14).

Q-101   What is the legal status of the Uniform Guidelines on Employee Selection Procedures?

First, the *Uniform Guidelines*, which were published in 1978, represent the latest in a series of attempts to develop a set of uniform standards that different federal agencies could use in carrying out their responsibilities of prohibiting employment discrimination. Between 1966 and 1978, there have been 6 different federal testing guidelines or orders: The shelf life of these guidelines has historically not been very long. Second, the *Uniform Guidelines* represent a mixture of administrative and technical provisions governing the use of tests and other selection devices in the workplace.

Based on the relevant rulings of the Supreme Court, the exact legal status of federal testing guidelines seems to be undergoing a metamorphosis of its own. In *Griggs v. Duke Power Company* (3 FEP 175 (1971)), a unanimous Supreme Court regarded the 1970 EEOC guidelines on employment testing procedures as "entitled to great deference," "expressing the will of Congress," and "comporting with Congressional intent." In *Albemarle Paper Co. v. Moody* (10 FEP 1181 (1975)), the majority of the Supreme Court justices cited specific provisions in the 1970 EEOC guidelines to fault the validation study offered by Albemarle Paper Company in defense of its tests. In a dissenting opinion, Chief Justice Burger cautioned against what he termed "slavish adherence to the EEOC Guidelines." In *Washington v. Davis* (12 FEP 1415 (1976)), the Supreme Court took exception to the EEOC guidelines' preference for criterion-related validation for demonstrating that tests are job related by ruling that the 3 professionally acceptable ways of test validation (content, construct, and criterion related) are equally appropriate under the proper circumstances.

The message from the different Supreme Court opinions seems to be that while the exact legal status of the EEOC guidelines is indeterminate, the guidelines are not to be taken lightly. The courts will continue to accord the EEOC guidelines a degree of deference that warrants the advice that prudent decision makers would do well to abide by the EEOC guidelines whenever feasible.

TO TEST OR NOT TO TEST:
A QUESTION OF MANAGEMENT

This book concludes with a section that pulls together the dominant theme of the book using a narrative format that departs from the question-and-answer pattern of the last several pages.

The title of this section is not intended to suggest that the question of whether to use tests in the employment setting has reached crisis proportions of the magnitude that Hamlet confronted. Some practitioners may disagree and point to the slings and arrows of numerous governmental regulations, the successive guidelines on employee selection procedures, the unsettled case law, and the technical jargon of psychologists and statisticians that has been known to baffle the likes of Odysseus.

OUR PITCH

Employment testing is a management tool for meeting the human resources requirements of the business. In the realities of today's world, this translates into 2 requirements: A test must measure job-relevant characteristics in order for the test user to identify job candidates with a high probability of doing well once on the job and use of the test must not interfere with the discharge of the test user's corporate responsibilities, including those that have to do with meeting affirmative action commitments.

The first requirement is technical in nature and is most usually associated with the concept of validation. Test validation, already an arduous professional undertaking, has become even more burdensome when it is conducted to the specifications of the *Uniform Guidelines on Employee Selection Procedures.* The second requirement is a federally mandated condition of doing business spawned by the passage of the Civil Rights Act of 1964 and its associated paraphernalia. Both requirements are operative and very compelling for all but the smallest businesses.

Because of known minority-majority group differences in the human condition, it is generally believed that the 2 requirements—of using tests to assess job qualifications, on the one hand, and of meeting affirmative action targets, on the other—are mutually exclusive. Some organizations have given up their testing programs so that they may meet their minority hiring requirements. There is at least 1 organization, however, that has demonstrated on a fairly massive scale that it is possible to comply with the terms of a consent decree requiring the accelerated utilization of women and minorities without giving up its testing program. American Telephone and Telegraph Company's chairman, Charles Brown,, attributed the Bell System's successful experience to a business-like approach: "We set about—as good business practice requires—developing the methods and procedures, the management instructions, the measurement plans and the tracking procedures—in short, the routines to assure that the job got done."

It takes effective and disciplined management to juggle the twin responsibilities successfully in the service of meeting the human resources requirements of the business. As noted in the preface, after the dust settles and group differences in test performance—their origins and consequences—have been studied, quantified, and litigated, it remains for competent management to "take it from here." To test or not to test is less a question *for* management than it is a question *of* management. As management steps up to the challenge, there are a number of distractors and harsh realities that need to be recognized.

DISTRACTORS

Distractors or decoys, in the terminology of psychometricians who develop multiple-choice tests, refer to response options that are plausible but incorrect. The status of distractors derives from their ability to attract the attention of the uninformed. In this book, distractors refer to those misconceptions about psychological measurement in general and employment testing in particular that have a nagging way of hanging on, well past their half-life. They have the status of myths. In the previous sections, there was occasion to dispose of some of them. In this section, a parting shot is taken at those distractors that seem particularly unhelpful to the managerial perspective urged in this book.

1. Freudian fixation on the origins of group differences in test performance. It is fairly clear by now that there are definite differences in test performance between minority and nonminority examinee groups. The observed differences have sparked the debate over whether the differences are due to genetic or environmental factors. The debate over the origins of group differences in test performance is interesting but largely peripheral to the business of running the business. The manager with personnel requisitions to fill has no control over the chromosomal endowment of his applicant pool nor does he have a say over the lifelong history of reinforcement that shaped the present behavior of his potential employees. He has to work with what he's got. His best chance at intervention lies in recognizing group differences when he commits corporate resources and support systems to those discretionary choices that have to do with enhancing the collective and individual competencies of the organization's human stock.

2. Overinterpretation of test scores. Among test-loving peoples who rely on test scores for many of life's important choices, there is a danger of imputing some magical property to test performance. R. Flaugher (1978) describes the tendency toward overinterpretation this way: "It is a great leap from being unable to work a few problems on a paper-and-pencil test to being declared lacking in 'practical judgment.'"

3. Equating group differences with test bias. It is commonly thought that a test is biased if minorities score lower on it than nonminorities. Stated differently, a test is fair if all groups test out the same way. An employment test may be regarded as a measuring instrument and as an instrument of prediction. As a measuring device, the test registers individual and group differences in qualifications. As an instrument of prediction, the test is a personnel tool for identifying job candidates who are most likely to do well on the job.

Defining test bias solely in terms of test performance looks only at the measuring function of the test and overlooks its use as a predictor of job performance. Because tests are used in the employment context to select candidates who have a high probability of performing well on the job, the determination of the test's fairness must go beyond differences in test performance to take in differences in job performance. Issues pertaining to test fairness must address the question of whether a job candidate's probability of successfully performing the job is commensurate with the probability of his being selected for the job. Thus, group differences in test performance, without more data, are not sufficient to establish that a test is biased or unfair. When appropriate research designs are employed to investigate the question of test bias, the general finding has been that tests are valid for and fair to minorities and nonminorities alike.

4. Validity based on N = *1.* Question 51 captures the essence of this misconception: "Suppose a company hires Joe on the basis of his high scores on a validated pre-employment test. Joe, however, does not work out on the job. What does this say about the validity of the test?"

Establishing the validity of a test involves the participation of a number of study subjects whose performance on the test is correlated with their subsequent behavior on the job. The behavior of any 1 person, during the validation study or after it, provides little information on the test's validity. Furthermore, since no test is perfectly valid, there will be occasional "misses": persons whose job behavior does not track with their test scores. It is frequently these persons who catch the eye; those who contribute to test validity by performing on the job in accordance with what their test scores indicate are playing by the rules and are therefore not as noticeable as the exceptions.

The tendency to notice the exceptions and to be overly impressed by them is not unique to employment testing. In the medical field, the most competent doctor is sued for malpractice, not for 999 successful operations, but for that 1 incidence of professional inadvertence.

5. Validity by visual inspection. It is not an uncommon tactic to visually examine the items comprising a test for their apparent correspondence with what the job requires as a way of determining whether the test is valid. Using this strategy, a test is dismissed as invalid if it contains items asking examinees to identify the next figure in a series of geometric designs when the job requires no abstract reasoning.

The process of establishing test validity by visual inspection would entrust the fundamental soundness of a testing program—its job relatedness—to the eye of the beholder and a test would have as many validities as there are viewers. Establishing a test's validity requires methodologies more rigorous than the "eyeball" approach.

HARSH REALITIES

In addition to the distractors listed above, employment testing is embedded in a number of harsh, unyielding realities that are detailed below.

1. Reality and consequences of group differences in test performance. It is noted above that there are group differences in test performance between minority and nonminority examinees. These differences are real, not artifacts of the data or statistical abstractions. For minority job candidates who must compete in a culture other than their own, the differences can quickly and decisively turn into handicaps that have implications for their daily bread. For the legal profession, group differences in test performance form the basis for a showing of adverse impact and the attendant need to reach the question of the test's job relatedness. For the manager who uses tests not to register group differences in test scores but to make selection decisions, the job of filling vacancies with qualified personnel without missing EEO targets becomes more complicated in the face of these group differences in test performance.

2. The need to make selection decisions. Managers who are faced with making selection decisions in which many are called but only a few can be chosen will make these decisions with or without the benefit of employment tests. The need to fill personnel requisitions in a timely fashion cannot be held in abeyance until the ultimate version of the government's guidelines on employee selection procedures is recorded in the *Federal Register.* The manager's realities are now.

3. EEO laws are here to stay. Few events have changed the landscape of the personnel manager's turf as drastically and as pervasively as the emergence of EEO laws—a whole host of them enacted at various levels of government. It is not likely that there will be any significant retreat from the policy that employment decisions of various sorts should be based on a person's ability to do the job, not on accidents of birth such as age, race, sex, color, or national origin.

4. Validity is the bottom line. Professionals have long recognized the need for validation as a threshold requirement to ensure that selection decisions are based on job-relevant standards. Validation makes good business sense as well because it provides credible information about a job candidate's likely job performance before the person is selected for the job. Furthermore, conventional employment tests enjoy a variety of psychometric and administrative advantages over alternative selection procedures. Validation makes even more sense in today's contemporary climate as a defense against charges of discriminatory employment practices. There is more to employment testing than a stopwatch, a few test booklets, and a supply of machine-scorable answer sheets. The days of installing a testing program out of a sense that it is the fashionable thing to do "to keep up with the Joneses" should be behind us. The potential legal exposure is great and the potential damage to the employment opportunities of minority applicants should touch the moral conscience of the most fashion conscious. But, above all, an invalid test represents an irrelevant source of difficulty.

Time to look beyond the distractors and the realities. To put the managerial perspective in better focus, examined here are things psychometric and things legalistic.

OF THINGS PSYCHOMETRIC

Validation has traditionally been the exclusive domain of psychologists and psychometricians. Developing selection procedures that measure relevant job requirements is one piece of the action; the other piece involves using the test to meet the human resources requirements of the business in harmony with the test user's affirmative action commitments. The point of view expressed here urges that both pieces of the action be factored into the set of business-like programs that are designed and structured to work.

As a first step, psychometric technicians and specialists are urged to consider talking in plainer English. As P. Crosby (1979) observed:

Professionals in any role who obscure explanations by using mysterious terminology do themselves, and their roles, a disservice. They get some satisfaction from seeing obvious confusion in the face of their superiors, but that confusion just makes everybody's job harder. (p. 3)

Secondly, it is not difficult for the psychometrician to be so enamored with the data that he loses sight of the broader reality. Validation, for example, is more than a laboratory exercise in collecting data for the purpose of testing hypotheses about the relationship between test performance and job performance. It is an organizational happening, with practical implications for the manner in which the resources of the organization are to be structured in order to satisfy the requirements of the study and to implement the results. In the second section of this book, validation concepts were discussed from both the technical and the practical points of view in an attempt to link the world of the researcher and the world of the practitioner. The judgment is not that one is seemingly more mundane than the other. The belief is that both are relevant. As a general posture, then, we believe it is a worthwhile and profitable objective for the researcher to be more attuned to the needs of the sponsoring client, to become more of a team player than a technical recluse.

It is quite clear that advances in the psychometric arena have increased our understanding of the technical considerations underlying questions of social policy and business practice. If it seems that this book is demanding more, it is out of the conviction that more can be done.

OF THINGS LEGALISTIC

The contemporary scene is one in which every personnel decision is potentially a legal transaction protected by one EEO law or another. Under the circumstances, it is not difficult to understand why the legal presence in traditionally personnel functions has increased. The role of things legalistic is examined in 2 scenarios: within the context of a discrimination lawsuit and within the context of the day-to-day running of the business. In both contexts, legal considerations should serve to focus, not distort, business priorities.

In the area of employment testing litigation, the general ground rules are fairly clear for handling situations that have escalated into discrimination lawsuits. Two propositions capture the fundamentals of the case law:

A. Employment tests that have an adverse impact on classes protected by Title VII, even though neutral on their face and neutral in intent, must be shown to be job related to survive challenge.
B. Job relatedness of employee selection procedures is shown by competent validity evidence obtained from a study conducted along the lines spelled out in governmental guidelines on testing.

With respect to the daily routine of making employment decisions, should legal considerations be the tail that wags the dog or vice versa? As pointed out earlier, it will be a sad day when the personnel manager abdicates his decision-making prerogatives to his lawyer or when the legal department is seduced into running the employment office.

OF THINGS MANAGERIAL

There was a time in the not too distant past when employment testing was the exclusive domain of psychologists and test validation was a scientific but isolated activity. Lapses in the design of validity studies jeopardized the chances of getting the studies published in some professionally refereed journal.

With the passage of the Civil Rights Act of 1964, employment testing became a multidisciplinary enterprise that entailed some opportunities and risks for those involved in it. The substantive developments of the last several years showed growing pains: The developments were generated by and for specialists and they focused on the more procedural/mechanical aspects of EEO as it relates to employment testing. Thus, bureaucrats channeled their energies in developing a succession of federal guidelines on testing, each generation designed to be both an enforcement tool and a guide for practitioners. Statisticians were drawn into the action to develop formulae and formulations for quantifying the adverse impact of selection procedures. Lawyers and judges buttoned down the order and allocation of burden of proof, the jurisdictional prerequisites to a lawsuit and the interrelationships among various sources of protection. Throughout this period, it seemed as though just about everyone has had a crack at influencing events. Everyone but the test user.

Going back to basics, it occurs to us that the ultimate user of validated products is the manager. Not only must he use tests to achieve the business objective of managing applicant flow and of selecting the best qualified, he is also held accountable for managing the adverse impact that results from the application of the validated devices. Ultimately, tests are tools and people make the decisions. This reality seems to have gotten lost in the heated debate over the origins of group differences in test performance; it seems to have been overlooked in the technician's zeal to structure his validity studies to be in compliance with the *Uniform Guidelines on Employee Selection Procedures.*

Putting it together, making things happen are expressions that capture management's unique charge to use tests responsibly so that he derives the benefits of job relatedness as he manages the by-product (adverse impact) of test use. This is a point of view that goes beyond the mechanics of test validation. It is a perspective that places a higher value on human resource utilization than on utilization of testing devices.

The transition to the managerial perspective will present some with what Pogo characterized as "insurmountable opportunities." Most rites of passage do. But for Pogo and for most of us, the future is not what it used to be!

GLOSSARY OF TERMS

Adverse impact: Refers to the uneven effects or consequences that result from the application of a selection procedure and is reflected, for example, in disparities in passing rates or selection rates between minority and nonminority applicants. A particular selection procedure may be neutral on its face and may be administered in a uniform fashion to all job candidates but still have an adverse impact if proportionately more minority examinees fail the test than their nonminority counterparts.

American Psychological Association (APA): The national organization for psychologists with a membership of approximately 50,000. The APA has 35 divisions representing different specialty areas within the field of psychology.

Base rate: Refers to the relative incidence of a given behavior in the population. Within the context of determining the practical utility of a validated test, the base rate refers to the proportion of employees who are satisfactory performers on the job prior to the implementation of a validated test. The base rate is a benchmark for gauging the amount of improvement that is attributable to the test's use.

Central tendency: Refers to the tendency exhibited by the conservative rater who "plays it safe" by displacing his judgments toward the center of the scale, avoiding ratings in either the favorable or the unfavorable direction.

Civil Rights Act of 1964: The federal law, enacted in 1964 and amended in 1972, which prohibits discrimination on the basis of race, sex, color, religion, or national origin in a wide range of decisions or transactions including those made in educational, housing, and employment contexts.

Class action lawsuit: A lawsuit brought by an aggrieved person on behalf of himself and of others who are similarly situated. The class action lawsuit is seen as an efficient mechanism for avoiding duplicate trials for resolving multiple controversies that involve essentially the same facts, issues, defenses, and questions of law.

Concurrent validity: The validity obtained when employees on the payroll (as opposed to applicants for employment) are used as study subjects in a criterion-related validation study. To the extent that present employees may not be representative of the typical applicant population in terms of their test and/or criterion performance, restriction of range may occur, resulting in lowered validity coefficients.

Construct validation: One of 3 professionally acceptable ways of showing the job relatedness of a selection procedure, construct validation involves a showing that the selection procedure in question measures the construct or trait (such as mechanical aptitude) and that the construct is involved in the performance of the job to a significant degree.

Correlation: A concept that refers to the extent to which 2 items or variables tend to vary together or to be associated with each other. The reported correlation between height and weight, for example, expresses the general observation that taller people tend to weigh more than shorter ones. (The fact that there are some shorter people who weigh more than some taller people indicates that the correlation between height and weight, although substantial, is not perfect.)

Correlation coefficient: A single number, ranging in value from -1.00 to $+1.00$, that summarizes the statistical relationship between 2 variables. The coefficient has 2 components: the absolute value that indicates the strength of the relationship and the sign—positive or negative—that indicates the direction of the relationship.

Criterion: The generic name for measures of job performance that are correlated with test scores in a validation study. Criteria of job performance are important in their own right: They represent those aspects of an organization's functioning that validated tests are intended to predict and maximize.

Criterion contamination: When supervisory evaluations are used as criterion measures of job performance in a criterion-related validation study, criterion contamination refers to the extent to which a supervisor's evaluations are influenced by knowledge of his subordinate's test scores. Criterion contamination resembles a self-fulfilling prophecy since the supervisor rates his subordinates low or high based on the subordinates' test performance rather than based on their job performance.

Cross-validation: The process involved in checking the stability of statistical weights to apply to tests in a battery or to items and item alternatives found to differentiate between known criterion groups. Procedurally, cross-validation involves applying the prediction system developed in 1 sample to the scores of another, independent sample, in order to answer the question: Are study outcomes from Sample A generalizable to Sample B?

Differential validity: Refers to the hypothesis that a test has different meanings for different subgroups either because the test is valid for Group A (for example, whites) but not for Group B (for example, blacks) or because the test is significantly more valid for Group A than for Group B.

Disparate treatment: The form of discrimination that involves treating members of one group (for example, males) differently from members of another group (for example, females). In a testing scenario, disparate treatment may consist of giving male examinees extra time to complete the test than is called for by the test directions while holding female examinees to the prescribed time limits.

Division 14: The Division of Industrial and Organizational Psychology within the American Psychological Association. The development and validation of selection procedures are prominent activities among members of Division 14.

Equal Employment Opportunity Commission (EEOC): The federal agency created by Title VII of the Civil Rights Act of 1964 to administer the antidiscrimination provisions of that title.

Executive Order 11246: The Executive Order signed by President Johnson in 1965 and amended by Executive Order 11375 that prohibits employment discrimination based on race, color, religion, national origin, or sex on the part of contractors doing business with the federal government.

Expectancy chart/table: A graphical or tabular representation of the outcome of a validation study that shows the proportion of successful employees meeting a certain standard of job performance at various score levels of the test.

Face validity: Refers to the extent to which a test appears valid to those who take the test, administer the test, or to the decision maker who will act upon test results. Although face validity is neither a technical aspect of validity nor a professional requirement, it has implications for how well the testing program will be accepted or remain credible in the eyes of the nontechnical person.

Halo: Refers to the tendency to give an individual the same rating on a number of specific performance dimensions (for example, quality of work, interpersonal relationships) because of an overall general impression.

Leniency: Refers to the tendency to displace one's ratings toward either the favorable or the unfavorable end of the rating scale. Some raters are "soft" and assign mostly favorable ratings, while others are "hard-boiled" and give predominantly unfavorable ratings.

Multiple correlation: When 2 or more tests are found to be valid, their use in combination results in an increase in the accuracy of prediction. The relationship between performance on the composite battery of tests and the criterion of job performance is known as the multiple correlation.

Multiple cutoff: Refers to that strategy for using tests in combination that involves setting critical cutoff scores on each test in the battery. The examinee who fails to reach the minimum level set for a test is rejected from further consideration. Put another way: In order to be included in the test-qualified pool, a job candidate must meet or exceed the cutoff scores on all the tests. Unlike the compensatory philosophy embodied in the multiple regression concept, the multiple cutoff strategy assumes that a deficiency in 1 test can not be made up by outstanding performance in another test.

Multiple regression: A statistical technique used to determine the optimum weighting scheme to apply to a battery of tests in order to achieve the best prediction of the criterion of job performance. In general, the weight that a particular test receives depends on 2 considerations: the test's zero-order validity—how well the test predicts the criterion by itself; and the test's intercorrelations with other tests—how much the test overlaps with other tests. The multiple regression approach to the use of tests in combination reflects a compensatory view in the sense that qualification standards are based on the total test battery. Thus, the person who does poorly on 1 component of the battery may make up for it by doing very well on the rest of the test battery.

Predictive validity: Refers to the validity obtained when applicants for employment (rather than present employees already working in the job being studied) are used as study subjects in a criterion-related validation study.

Predictor: The generic name for tests and other selection devices that are validated for the purpose of determining whether they are predictive of the likely job behavior of job candidates.

Rater tendencies: When supervisory evaluations of their subordinates are used as criterion measures of job performance, the evaluative judgments are frequently registered by the use of rating scales. Rater tendencies refer to consistent tendencies to systematically displace one's judgments toward selected portions of the rating scale. Halo, leniency, and central tendency are the most common rater tendencies.

Reliability: Refers to the extent to which a test is precise or free of error so that repeated measurements yield consistent results. The reliability of a test is usually estimated by correlating 2 comparable forms of the same test or by correlating the scores obtained by administering the same test twice. The more reliable the test, the more closely the numerical value of the coefficient comes to 1.00.

Restriction of range: When a particular test has been used to select sample members participating in the validation study, a restriction of range in test scores will characterize the sample since low-scoring applicants will presumably have been rejected. A similar restriction of range phenomenon will characterize the criterion measure of job performance when the better employees are promoted or when the unsatisfactory ones are terminated and neither are included in the validation study sample. The validity coefficient computed on a sample with a restricted range of scores on either the predictor and/or the criterion variables will underestimate the true validity of the test.

Selection ratio: Refers to the number of persons selected relative to the number of applicants. The smaller the selection ratio, the more selective the test user can be in "skimming the cream" and the higher the practical gains that will accrue from the implementation of a valid test.

Significance levels: Refer to the levels of risk of making incorrect inferences about characteristics of the population based on sample results. The conventional significance levels are 5% and 1%. A validity coefficient of .45 is said to be significant at the 1% level if the risks are only 1 in 100 that in the population from which the particular sample was drawn, no relationship in fact exists between performance on the test and performance on the criterion measure of job performance. If no relationship exists between test and job performance in the population, the likelihood of obtaining a correlation as big as or bigger than .45 in the sample is about 1 in 100.

Significance testing: Significance testing is a statistical procedure for estimating the probable fluctuations that can be expected from sample to sample so that inferences can be drawn about characteristics of populations in light of sample results.

Standardization: Refers to uniformity of procedure in administering the test and scoring test results. Test scores should reflect individual differences in skills and abilities rather than differences in testing conditions.

Taylor-Russell tables: A series of tables that show the practical utility of tests for different combinations of test validity, base rate, and selection ratio.

Test fairness: Questions about test fairness center on whether and the extent to which a person's probability of being successful on the job is commensurate with the probability of his being selected for the job. Test fairness is not an inherent property of the test but is evaluated by examining whether the test's operational use to make selection decisions consistently underpredicts or overpredicts the job performance of certain groups of examinees.

Title VII of the Civil Rights Act: That section of the Civil Rights Act that prohibits discrimination on the basis of race, sex, color, national origin, or religion in the employment context.

Uniform Guidelines on Employee Selection Procedures: The document that provides guidance on the use of tests and other employee selection procedures and that was promulgated in September 1978 by various agencies of the federal government (Equal Employment Opportunity Commission, Civil Service Commission, Department of Justice and Department of Labor) charged with implementing equal employment opportunity policies.

Utility: Refers to the practical gains that can be expected to flow from the use of a test. The gains are dependent on 3 items: the test's validity (the higher the test validity, the greater the utility); selection ratio (the more selective the test user, the lower the selection ratio and the higher the utility); and base rate (the closer the base rate is to .50, the higher the utility).

REFERENCES

American Psychological Association. *Standards for Educational and Psychological Tests and Manuals.* Washington, D.C.: American Psychological Association, 1966.

American Psychological Association. *Standards for Educational and Psychological Tests.* Washington, D.C.: American Psychological Association, 1974.

American Psychological Association. Division of Industrial-Organizational Psychology. *Principles for the Validation and Use of Personnel Selection Procedures.* 2d ed. Berkeley: Calif.: Division of Industrial-Organizational Psychology, 1980.

BNA Survey. *Employee Selection Procedures.* Personnel Policies Forum Survey no. 70. Washington, D.C.: Bureau of National Affairs, 1963.

Brogden, H. "On the interpretation of the correlation coefficient as a measure of predictive efficiency." *Journal of Educational Psychology* 37 (1946): 65-76.

Brown, C. *"What more is there to say?"* A talk before the National Urban League Conference. New York, August 5, 1980.

Callender, J., and Osburn, H. G. "Development and test of a new model for validity generalization." *Journal of Applied Psychology* 65 (1980): 543-558.

Cronbach, L., and Gleser, G. *Psychological Tests and Personnel Decisions.* Urbana: University of Illinois Press, 1965.

Crosby, P. *Quality is Free.* New York: McGraw-Hill, 1979.

Division of Industrial-Organizational Psychology, APA. *Principles for the*

Validation and Use of Personnel Selection Procedures. Dayton, Ohio: Industrial-Organizational Psychologist, 1975.

Equal Employment Opportunity Commission, Office of Personnel Management, Department of Justice, Department of Labor. Adoption of questions and answers to clarify and promote a common interpretation of the uniform guidelines on employee selection procedures. *Federal Register*, 44 (1979): 11996-12009.

Flaugher, R. "The many definitions of test bias." *American Psychologist* 33 (1978): 671-679.

Friedman, T., and Williams, E. B. *Current Use of Tests for Employment: A Report to the Committee on Ability Testing, National Academy of Sciences.* (Prepublication draft.) Princeton, N.J.: Educational Testing Service, 1980.

Gardner, J. *Excellence.* New York: Harper and Row, 1961.

Ghiselli, E. *The Validity of Occupational Aptitude Tests.* New York: Wiley, 1966.

Gross, M. *The Brain Watchers:* New York: Random House, 1962.

Hoffman, B. *The Tyranny of Testing.* New York: Crowell-Collier, 1962.

Jensen, A. *Bias in Mental Testing.* New York: Free Press, 1980.

Manese, W. R. *Employment Testing, Validation and the Law—A Primer.* Berkeley Heights, N.J.: EGM Enterprises, 1979.

Meehl, P. *Clinical versus Statistical Prediction: A Theoretical Analysis.* Minneapolis: University of Minnesota Press, 1954.

Miner, M. *Selection Procedures and Personnel Records.* Personnel Policies Forum Survey no. 114. Washington, D.C.: Bureau of National Affairs, 1976.

Naylor, J., and Shine, L. "A table for determining the increase in mean criterion score obtained by using a selection device." *Journal of Industrial Psychology* 3 (1965): 33-42.

Personnel Research and Development Corporation. *Equal Employment Opportunity: An Interpretive Guide.* Washington, D.C.: American Petroleum Institute, 1972.

Popham, W. *Criterion-Referenced Measurement.* Englewood Cliffs, N.J.: Prentice-Hall, 1978.

Prentice-Hall, Inc. *P-H Survey: Employee Testing and Selection Procedures— Where Are They Headed?* Englewood Cliffs, N.J.: Prentice-Hall, 1975.

Reilly, R. R., and Chao, G. "Validity and fairness of some alternative employee selection procedures." *Personnel Psychology* 35 (1982): 1-62.

Schaie, K. "Age changes in adult intelligence." In D. S. Woodruff and J. Birren, eds., *Aging: Scientific Perspectives and Social Issues.* New York: Van Nostrand, 1975.

Schaie, K., and Lavouvie-Vief, G. "Generational versus ontogenetic components of change in cognitive behavior: A fourteen-year cross-sequential study." *Developmental Psychology* 10 (1974): 305-320.

Schlei, B., and Grossman, P. *Employment Discrimination Law.* Washington, D.C.: Bureau of National Affairs, 1976.

Schmidt, F., and Hunter, J. "Development of a general solution to the problem of validity generalization." *Journal of Applied Psychology* 62 (1977): 529-540.

Schmidt, F., and Hunter, J. "Employment testing: Old theories and new research findings." *American Psychologist* 36 (1981): 1128-1137.

Schmidt, F.; Hunter, J.; McKenzie, R.; and Muldrow, T. "The impact of valid selection procedures on workforce productivity." *Journal of Applied Psychology* 64 (1979): 609-626.

Schmidt, F.; Hunter, J.; Pearlman, K,; and Shane, G. "Further tests of the Schmidt-Hunter Bayesian validity generalization procedure." *Personnel Psychology* 32 (1979): 257-281.

Schmidt, F.; Hunter, J.; and Urry, V. "Statistical power in criterion-related validity studies." *Journal of Applied Psychology* 61 (1976): 473-485.

Taylor, H., and Russell, J. "The relationship of validity coefficients to the practical effectiveness of tests in selection: Discussion and tables." *Journal of Applied Psychology* 23 (1939): 565-578.

U.S. Equal Employment Opportunity Commission, U.S. Civil Service Commission, U.S. Department of Labor, and U.S. Department of Justice. "Uniform Guidelines on Employee Selection Procedures." *Federal Register* 43, 166 (1978): 38295-38309.

Williams, R. "Black pride, academic relevance and individual achievement." *The Consulting Psychologist* 2 (1970): 18-22.

INDEX

About the Author

WILFREDO R. MANESE, PH.D., a well-known authority on testing and testing litigation, is Director of Human Resources Research and Applications at Northwestern Bell. He has served as a consultant for both industry and government and has taught courses in industrial psychology, testing, and measurement. His articles and reports in the field of employment testing have appeared in scholarly and industrial publications.